D0019124

ALSO BY BRUCE PANDOLFINI
IN THE FIRESIDE CHESS LIBRARY:

Let's Play Chess
Bobby Fischer's Outrageous Chess Moves
One-Move Chess by the Champions
Principles of the New Chess
The ABC's of Chess
Kasparov's Winning Chess Tactics
Russian Chess
*The Best of Chess Life & Review, Volumes I
    and II* (editor)
Pandolifini's Endgame Course
Chess Openings: Traps and Zaps
Square One
Weapons of Chess
Chessercizes
More Chessercizes: Checkmate!
Pandolfini's Chess Complete

BEGINNING CHESS

BRUCE PANDOLFINI

A FIRESIDE BOOK
PUBLISHED BY SIMON & SCHUSTER
New York London Toronto Sydney Tokyo Singapore

FIRESIDE

Rockefeller Center
1230 Avenue of the Americas
New York, New York 10020

Copyright © 1993 by Bruce Pandolfini

All rights reserved
including the right of reproduction
in whole or in part in any form.

FIRESIDE and colophon are registered trademarks
of Simon & Schuster Inc.

Designed by Stanley S. Drate/Folio Graphics Co. Inc.
Manufactured in the United States of America

10   9   8   7

Library of Congress Cataloging in Publication Data
Pandolfini, Bruce.
    Beginning chess / Bruce Pandolfini.
        p.   cm.
    "A Fireside book."
    Includes index.
    1. Chess. 2. Chess problems. I. Title.
GV1446.P337   1993
794.1—dc20   93-9693
                                    CIP

ISBN: 0-671-79501-5

For the Waitzkins,
Fred and Bonnie,
Josh and Katya

CONTENTS

Acknowledgments

I would like to thank Roselyn Abrahams,
Bruce Alberston, Carol Ann Caronia, Deirdre Hare,
Burt Hochberg, Bonni Leon, David MacEnulty,
Idelle Pandolfini, Judy Shipman, Nick Viorst, and my
editor Kara Leverte for putting this book together
and making it much better.

PREFACE

Beginning Chess is a book of chess tactics for newcomers and intermediate players. It offers three hundred problems in thirty tests of ten problems each. Eleven different tactical themes are featured—forks, pins, skewers, discoveries, underminings, x-rays, traps, overloads, promotions and underpromotions, *en prise* captures, and direct checkmates—the stratagems that occur most often in friendly and offhand games.

There are other tactical chess books on the market. What makes *Beginning Chess* different is its simplicity. Every problem can be answered in one move. No problem has more than ten pieces on the board. Pieces are arranged in clear patterns, easily remembered. Each problem has only one correct idea. Diligent first-time players can actually solve them.

The book is divided into three sections: instruction, tests, and answers. The first part offers a brief, but sufficiently full introduction to the moves and rules of chess. It also provides an explanation of the tactics that follow in the tests. Beginners can start playing and testing immediately after reading this section. Intermediate players can jump to the tests and answers, though it can't hurt to go through the instruction. Even former world champion Mikhail Tal (1936–92) used to scour beginners' books for ideas! He must have had a good reason.

You can record your answers in the spaces provided next to each diagram, but you might prefer using a separate sheet of paper so you can retake the tests in the future. I encourage my students to continue to solve the same examples until they really know them. If you originally solved a problem in two minutes, do it in one minute the next time. Then cut it in half again. The faster the better.

Time to learn, solve, and play. It all starts in the first section.

Moves, Rules, and Tactics

HOW TO PLAY CHESS

1 INTRODUCTION

Chess is a game of skill that originated more than fifteen hundred years ago, probably in the Indus Valley between Persia and India. It has gone through many changes since then, but the object remains the same: to checkmate the enemy king. What this means and how it's done is explained in what follows.

2 THE CHESSBOARD

Chess is played by two people on a board of sixty-four squares, of which thirty-two are light and thirty-two are dark. There are eight rows of eight squares each. The squares appear in three kinds of rows: (1) ranks (horizontal rows); (2) files (vertical rows); and (3) diagonals (slanted rows of one color).

The battleground

3 THE FORCES

Each side starts with a force of sixteen units: eight pieces and eight pawns. The light-colored force is called White and the darker Black. The eight pieces consist of one king, one queen, two rooks, two bishops, and two knights. The eight pawns are not counted as pieces.

4 STARTING POSITION

The players sit on opposite sides of the board, next to their forces. Pieces occupy first ranks, pawns second ranks. There should be a light square in the near corner at each player's right. Remember the saying "light on the right." The same kinds of pieces begin on the same files. The queens start on squares of their own color, next to their respective kings. The White queen begins on the central light square, the Black queen on the central dark square. Remember the saying "queen on her own color." This works only if the board is placed correctly, with a light square on the right.

The starting position

5 GENERAL RULES

Players take turns moving their own armies, one unit per turn, in one direction per turn. White always moves first. Moves must conform to the rules. If a move violates a rule it is illegal and must be replaced with a legal move. Turns are completed by moving or capturing. A move is the transfer of a unit from one square to another. A capture is the replacement of an enemy unit by a friendly one (units are not jumped as they are in checkers). A captured unit is taken from the board and can no longer participate. No move or capture is compulsory unless it's the only legal play. Players capture enemy units, not their own. A unit may capture any enemy unit, if it's a legal move. Two units can never occupy the same square. Two units cannot be moved on the same turn (except when castling, which will be explained later), nor can two enemy units be captured on the same move. In the course of play, all sixty-four squares can be used for legal moves and captures.

6 THE KING

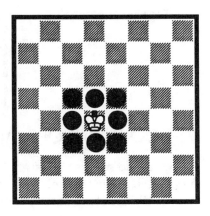

POSITION: **W: Kd4**

The king can move to any of the marked squares.

Each unit moves according to prescribed rules. Kings move or capture one square in any direction: horizontally, vertically, diagonally, backward, or forward. In capturing, they simply make their move and replace whatever occupies their destination square. They cannot move to squares where they can be captured.

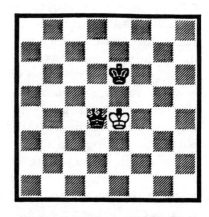

POSITION: W: Ke4
           B: Ke6 Qd4
BEFORE: **White's king can take the queen.**

POSITION: W: Kd4
           B: Ke6
AFTER: **The king has taken the queen.**

7 ROOKS, BISHOPS, AND QUEENS

Rooks move along ranks and files as far as desired until blocked by friendly or enemy units or the edge of the board. Obstructing enemy units may be captured. Bishops move only on diagonals of one color, forward or backward, as many unblocked squares as desired. If a bishop starts on a light square, it can never move to or capture on a dark square. The queen is like a rook and a bishop combined. It moves in any direction, as many unblocked squares as desired. Bishops and queens, like rooks, may capture obstructing enemy units if the move is legal.

IN EACH DIAGRAM, THE WHITE PIECE CAN MOVE TO ANY OF THE MARKED SQUARES.

POSITION: **W: Rd4**

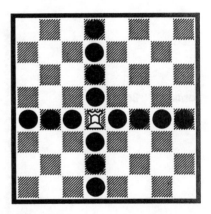

POSITION: **W: Ra1**

POSITION: **W: Bd4**

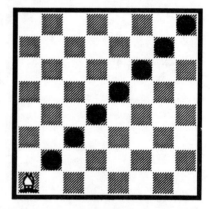

POSITION: **W: Ba1**

POSITION: **W: Qd4**

POSITION: **W: Qa1**

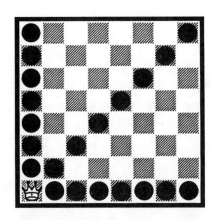

POSITION: **W: Rh1**
          B: Rh8 Ba8 Na1
White's rook may take the rook or the knight.

POSITION: **W: Ba1**
          B: Rh8 Ba8 Na1
White's bishop may take the bishop.

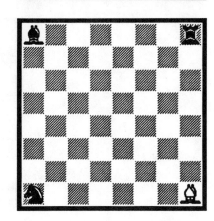

POSITION: **W: Qa1**
           B: Rh8 Ba8 Na1

White's queen may take any of Black's pieces.

8 THE KNIGHT

The knight does not move in straight lines, but it always makes a move of the same distance and design. Its move can be described in several ways. The usual way is to say that its move has two parts. It can go two squares along a rank or file, then one square at a right angle; or one square along a rank or file, then two squares at a right angle. The full move, from start to finish, backward or forward, left

THE KNIGHT CAN MOVE TO ANY OF THE MARKED SQUARES.

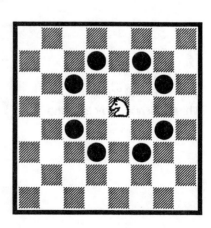

POSITION: **W: Ne5**

POSITION: **W: Na1**

POSITION: **W: Nd4**
       B: Rd5 Re4 Bc3 Nd3
       Pe3 Pc5 Pd5 Pe5

The knight can jump over obstacles. It can move to any of the marked squares.

POSITION: **W: Bd7 Nd5 Pc6**
       B: Rc7 Pc5 Pd6

The knight can take the rook.

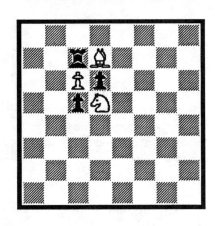

or right, looks like the capital letter L. On each move, the knight must land on a square of a different color from the one it started on. The knight makes its L-shaped moves and captures regardless of intervening friendly and enemy units. Nothing can block a knight. Knights are the only pieces that can move in the opening position because they can scale the obstructing pawns. Other pieces can't move until pawns are moved out of the way.

9 THE PAWN

Pawns are the only units that move one way and capture another. Also, they are the only units that can't move backward or to the side. They move one square straight ahead but capture one square *diagonally* ahead. They cannot capture straight ahead. Each pawn has an option on its first move: It can move either one or two squares forward. After its first move, it can never move two squares again, even if it didn't go two squares initially.

POSITION: **W: Pd2 Pf3**

The pawn on the left can move one or two squares. The pawn on the right can move just one square.

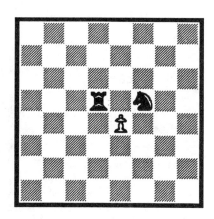

POSITION: **W: Pe4**
            B: Rd5 Nf5
The pawn can capture either piece.

10 CHECKMATE

The object of a chess game is to checkmate the enemy king. The king is checkmated when it is under direct attack (threatened by capture) and its capture on the next move cannot be prevented. The game ends at that point, without the actual capture taking place. If the king is attacked but can avoid capture, then it's merely in check, not checkmate.

POSITION: **W: Kc8 Bb7**
            B: Ka8
BY MOVING: The Black king can get out of check by moving to square a7.

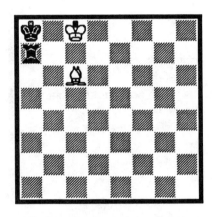

POSITION: **W: Kc8 Bc6**
        B: Ka8 Ra7
BY BLOCKING: **The rook can block the check.**

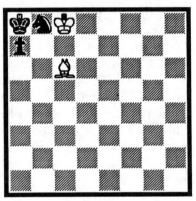

POSITION: **W: Kc8 Bc6**
        B: Ka8 Nb8 Pa7
BY CAPTURE: **The knight can capture the bishop.**

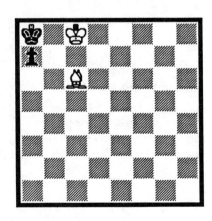

POSITION: **W: Kc8 Bc6**
        B: Ka8 Pa7
Black has been checkmated.

BLACK HAS BEEN CHECKMATED.

POSITION: **W: Kf6 Rd8**
         B: Kf8

POSITION: **W: Kf6 Qf7**
         B: Kf8

If your king is checked, you must get it out of check. There can be as many as three ways to get out of check. You can (1) capture the checking enemy unit; (2) block the check by putting a friendly unit in the way; or (3) move the king to safety, where it can't be captured. Any of these methods may be selected to end the check. If there is no way to stop the check, it's checkmate, or simply mate, and the game is over.

11 DRAWS

Sometimes neither player wins and the game is drawn. There are five ways a game can end in a draw: (1) agreement; (2) 50-move rule; (3) threefold repetition; (4) insufficient mating material; (5) stalemate. The first three methods are not relevant to this book because they will not help solve any of the given problems; the final two are.

A draw by agreement occurs when one side proposes a draw and the other accepts. A player can claim a draw by the 50-move rule if 50 moves have been played (50 for each side) without a pawn being moved or a unit captured. A player can claim a draw by threefold repetition if the same position and conditions occur three times. The repetitions do not have to happen on consecutive moves.

A game is drawn by insufficient mating material if neither player has enough material left to checkmate, even with the other side's cooperation. For example, a king and bishop can't beat a lone king. A king and rook, however, can force mate against a solitary king.

A game is drawn by stalemate if the side to move doesn't have a legal move with any unit but is not in check. Even

POSITION: **W: Kc8 Bb6**
      B: Ka8
Black has been stalemated.

if one side has a vast material superiority, it's still stalemate and the game is drawn if the other side is not in check but doesn't have a legal play. In fact, this is often a losing side's last hope: to lure the opponent into an accidental stalemate.

12 CHECK, CHECKMATE, AND STALEMATE

Just to review the distinctions: You are in check if your king is in direct attack but there is a way to get out of check. You are checkmated if your king is in direct attack (in check) and there is no way to get out of check. You are stalemated if you are not in check, but don't have a legal move.

13 CASTLING

Castling is the only time you can move two pieces on the same turn. If nothing occupies the squares between your king and one of your rooks, you may castle. Castling has two parts. You castle by: (1) moving your king two squares along the rank toward the rook; and (2) moving the rook next to the king on its other side. You can castle using either rook, provided nothing is in the way and neither the king nor castling rook has moved before. If you castle toward White's right, you castle kingside. If you castle toward White's left, you castle queenside.

There are three other restrictions. You can't castle if your king is in check, if your king would be in check after castling, or if in the act of castling the king has to pass over a square attacked by the enemy. You can't castle in check, into check, or through check. If you can get out of check without moving the king or rook, however, you may still castle on future moves, assuming the move is then legal.

POSITION: **W: Ke1 Rh1**
Before White castles kingside

POSITION: **W: Kg1 Rf1**
After White castles kingside

POSITION: **W: Ke8 Ra8**
Before Black castles
queenside

POSITION: **W: Kc8 Rd8**
After castling queenside

POSITION: **W: Ke1 Rh1 Pb2 Pc2**
        B: Bb4
White can't castle while in
check.

POSITION: **W: Ke1 Rh1**
        B: Bc4
White can't castle through
check.

POSITION: **W: Ke1 Rh1**
    B: Bd4
White can't castle into check.

14 PROMOTION

When a pawn reaches the last square on a file it must be promoted to either a queen, a rook, a bishop, or a knight. You can promote to a new queen even if you still have your original queen. Thus you can have two, three, or more queens, rooks, bishops, or knights, in any combination. The choice is yours. Usually, an extra queen is decisive. But sometimes it might be desirable to underpromote to a knight, especially if the knight gives immediate checkmate.

POSITION: **W: Pe7**
**Before the pawn advances to
the last rank.**

POSITION: **W: Pe8**

The pawn has just advanced to the last rank. The move isn't completed yet.

POSITION: **W: Qe8**

The pawn has been promoted to a queen.

POSITION: **W: Ne8**

The pawn could have been promoted to a knight instead (or to a rook or a bishop).

15   EN PASSANT

There's a special kind of capture that involves just pawns, one White and one Black. The pawns must occupy adjacent files. One pawn captures and the other is captured. The pawn that captures must be on its fifth rank (counting from its side of the board). The pawn to be captured must start on its second rank.

Let's say the capturing pawn (on its fifth rank) is White and the pawn to be captured (on its second rank) is Black. If the Black pawn uses its two-square first-move option so that after moving it occupies the same rank as White's pawn, it can be captured by the White pawn *en passant* ("in passing"). The White pawn takes the Black pawn as if it had moved only one square. *En passant* captures must be exercised on the first opportunity or the option is forfeited.

POSITION: **W: Pe5**
   B: Pd7
Before Black's pawn moves two squares.

POSITION: **W: Pe5**
            B: Pd5
After Black's pawn has moved
two squares.

POSITION: **W: Pd6**
After White has taken Black's
pawn *en passant*.

16 ALGEBRAIC NOTATION

In order to read chess books, including this one, it helps to
know algebraic notation. Notation is a way to record your
moves and games using letters and numbers. There are
two popular systems: the descriptive, used in many older
chess books; and the algebraic, used in most newer ones,
including *Beginning Chess*, and sanctioned by the U.S.
Chess Federation.

In the algebraic system, the board is viewed as an eight-by-eight grid. Every square has a unique name based on the intersection of a file and a rank. Files are lettered *a* through *h*, beginning from White's left. Ranks are numbered *1* through *8*, beginning from White's nearest rank. Squares are named by combining letters and numbers, the letter being lower case and written first. Thus, in the starting position, White's king occupies *e1* and Black's king occupies *e8*. All squares in the algebraic system are named from White's standpoint. The algebraic grid shown below indicates the names of all the squares. If you have trouble remembering them, I suggest you photocopy the grid and use it as a bookmark, so it's always handy whenever you need it.

BLACK

a8	b8	c8	d8	e8	f8	g8	h8
a7	b7	c7	d7	e7	f7	g7	h7
a6	b6	c6	d6	e6	f6	g6	h6
a5	b5	c5	d5	e5	f5	g5	h5
a4	b4	c4	d4	e4	f4	g4	h4
a3	b3	c3	d3	e3	f3	g3	h3
a2	b2	c2	d2	e2	f2	g2	h2
a1	b1	c1	d1	e1	f1	g1	h1

The algebraic grid. Every square has a unique name.

WHITE

17 SYMBOLS YOU SHOULD KNOW

In order to read the answers in this book, you need to know the following symbols:

K	king
Q	queen

R	rook
B	bishop
N	knight
−	moves to
×	captures
+	check
+ +	checkmate
0-0	castles kingside
0-0-0	castles queenside

Note that pawns are not identified by letter. If no indication of the moving unit is offered, it must be a pawn.

18 A SHORT CHESS GAME

Consider the shortest game possible, which is two moves for White and two for Black. It is diagramed on the next page. If each move were written independently, here's how it would look in this book:

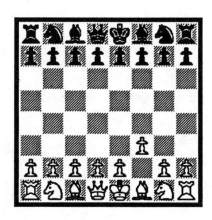

1. f2-f3 (White's first move)
White moves the pawn on f2 to f3.

1....e7-e5 (Black's first move)
Black moves the pawn on e7
to e5.

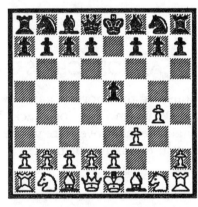

2. g2-g4 (White's 2nd move)
White moves the pawn on g2
to g4.

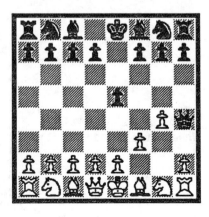

2....Qd8-h4 + + (Black's 2nd
move)
Black moves the queen on d8
to h4. This is checkmate.

19 HOW TO WIN CHESS GAMES

Most chess games are won in either of two ways: by checkmate or resignation. Players resign when mate appears inevitable. Resistance can seem futile when one falls behind in material, for the stronger force usually wins. Generally, material advantages are gained through immediate weapons called tactics.

There are many types of tactics in chess. *Beginning Chess* emphasizes those that are practical for newcomers and casual players. Once you know these tools you can begin to use them in your own games to win enemy units and get the better of exchanges. As a rule, try to give less than you get. To do this, it helps to know the values of the pieces. The following chart lists them, except for that of the king, which cannot be taken.

TABLE OF RELATIVE VALUES

Pawns	are worth	1	pawn
Knights	are worth	3	pawns
Bishops	are worth	3	pawns
Rooks	are worth	5	pawns
Queens	are worth	9	pawns

According to the chart, you should be willing to surrender a pawn for any piece; a knight or bishop for a rook or queen; a rook, bishop, or knight for a queen; a bishop and knight for a queen; a rook and knight or a rook and bishop for a queen; or a rook for a bishop and knight. Using this system as a guide, you can correctly analyze all the tactics occurring in the thirty tests of *Beginning Chess*. There are 11 different categories of tactics in this book. One is checkmate, in all its variety, which ends any game immediately. The other ten tactical themes primarily win material and therefore facilitate checkmate. They are illustrated in the following pages.

20   *EN PRISE*

A unit is *en prise* if it is unguarded and under direct attack so that it can be captured at no cost to the capturer. If a unit is *en prise* we say it is "hanging," or that it can be taken "for nothing" or "for free." All units can be *en prise* except the king, which can never be captured. In the diagram, whoever moves can take the other side's bishop for nothing.

POSITION: **W: Kd4 Bc1**
B: Ke6 Bh6
Whoever moves can take the other side's bishop for free.

21   FORK

You give a fork when one of your units attacks two or more enemy units with the same move. Sometimes only one of the enemy units can be saved, sometimes neither of them can. All units can fork. All can be forked. The diagram shows a knight forking Black's queen and rook. (In this diagram, and several others in the section, the kings are not shown to emphasize the concept.)

POSITION: **W: Nf7**
          B: Qd8 Rh8
The knight forks queen and
rook.

22 PIN

A pin is a straight-line tactic, usually involving three units:
an attacker and two defenders. The three units occupy the
same rank, file, or diagonal. The attacker threatens an
enemy unit that shields a more valuable enemy unit along
the line of attack. The unit closest to the attacking unit is
"pinned" to the unit behind it. Sometimes the shielding,

POSITION: **W: Bd3**
          B: Kh7 Re4
Black's rook is pinned and lost.

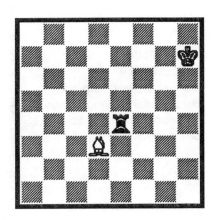

pinned unit is captured with material gain. In other cases, the pin renders the shielding unit helpless, so that it can be attacked and won by other attacking units. Queens, rooks, and bishops can pin. Any unit except the king can be pinned. In the diagram, the bishop is pinning the rook to the king. The rook can't be saved, even if it were Black's move.

23 SKEWER

The skewer is another straight-line tactic. Like a pin, it also involves one attacker and two defenders. But unlike a pin, the shielding defender is not frozen in place. Rather it is chased out of the way, exposing the defender behind it to capture. In a pin, the attacker is first in line, the less valuable defending unit is second, and the more valuable defending unit is third. In a skewer, the attacker is first, the more valuable defending unit is second, and the less valuable one is third. (For some skewers, the defending units are the same, such as two knights, or have the same

POSITION: W: Rf8
         B: Kf4 Bf1

The rook skewers king and bishop. After the king moves out of check, the bishop can be taken for free.

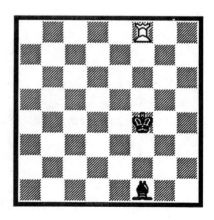

value, such as a bishop and knight.) Queens, rooks, and bishops can give skewers, and all units can be skewered. In the diagram, the rook skewers king and bishop. The king will have to move out of check and the bishop can be taken for free.

24 DISCOVERY

Another straight-line tactic is the discovery, or discovered attack. But unlike pins and skewers, it involves two attackers and only one defender along the primary line of aggression. One attacker moves, the other stays stationary. The moving unit unveils the stationary unit's attack on a defending unit. The stationary unit gives the discovered attack. A discovery to the king is a discovered check. Discoveries can be particularly potent when, in addition to the stationary unit, the moving unit also attacks. If both the moving and stationary units simultaneously check the enemy king, it's called double check, the deadliest weapon of all. Queens, rooks, and bishops can be the stationary

POSITION: **W: Re1 Be2**
           B: Ke7 Qa6 Pb5 Pc6
If the bishop moves, the rook gives discovered check.

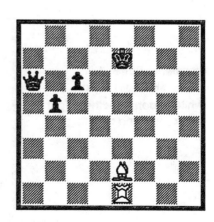

components in a discovery. Every unit except the queen can function as the moving attacker. Every unit can be exploited in a discovery, either by the stationary or moving attacker. In the diagram, the bishop can take the pawn at b5, attacking the queen. The queen couldn't then save itself because the rook is checking the king, giving it a discovered check. Since the king must be saved, the queen would be lost.

25 UNDERMINING

A unit is undermined when its protection is captured, driven away, or immobilized, such as by a pin. Then it can be captured for free. When a unit's protection is captured, usually by an even exchange, the tactic is also known as removing the defender or removing the guard. Any unit can undermine an enemy unit. All units except the king can be undermined. In the diagram, the defense of Black's knight is undermined when White's rook takes Black's. White's bishop then takes the knight for free.

POSITION: **W: Ra6 Bh3**
        B: Rd6 Nd7 Pc7
White undermines the knight by exchanging rook for rook.

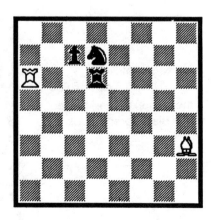

26 OVERLOAD

A unit is overloaded if it cannot fulfill all its defensive commitments. A typical instance is when a unit tries to guard two friendly units simultaneously. If one of the threatened units is taken, the defending unit is pulled out of position when it takes back. That leaves the other unit unguarded, to be taken for free. For example, suppose a pawn guards a bishop and knight, which are attacked by different enemy knights. The pawn is overloaded, because when the attacked knight is taken and the pawn takes back, the bishop is left unguarded and can be captured for free. All units can become overloaded. Every unit can be lost by an overload tactic, except the king. In the diagram, Black's pawn is overloaded, guarding both the bishop and the knight. White gains a piece by exchanging the bishop for the knight or the knight for the bishop, forcing the pawn out of position.

POSITION: **W: Be4 Nd4**
B: Be6 Nc6 Pd7
Black's pawn is overloaded.

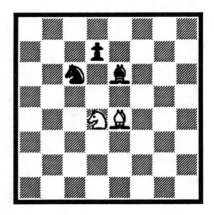

27 X-RAY

The basic x-ray (though not the only kind) involves two units of one color and one of the other, all three occupying and having the ability to move along the same line. A typical lineup would be (1) a White unit; (2) a Black unit; and (3) a White unit, in that order. If either White unit is captured by the Black unit, the other White unit could take back. Thus unit (1) defends unit (3), and unit (3) defends unit (1), even though unit (2) is in the middle. Units (1) and (3) provide x-ray support, in that they protect each other right through the Black unit. X-rays can be used in attack or defense. Queens and rooks can x-ray along ranks and files; queens and bishops along diagonals. The queen is particularly effective because it can merge attacking lines. So it can use a diagonal to join up with a rook, or a rank or file to converge with a bishop. In the diagram, White's rooks guard each other even with a Black rook in between.

POSITION: **W: Rd1 Rd8**
          B: Rd4
White's rooks protect each other through Black's rook.

28 TRAPPING

A piece is trapped if it doesn't have a safe move and can't adequately be protected. After trapping a piece, the idea is to win it by direct attack, capturing it for free or in exchange for a unit of lower value. If the lower-valued unit is then recaptured, the attacker (the trapper) still comes out ahead. Often the only recourse left to the trapped unit is to sell its life as dearly as possible, taking the most valuable unit in sight, even if only a pawn (at least it's something). Every unit can be trapped and won. When it happens to the king, the game is over by checkmate. In the diagram, the knight is trapped by the bishop and attacked by the rook. The knight is lost.

POSITION: **W: Rh8 Ba5**
     B: Na8
The knight is trapped and lost.

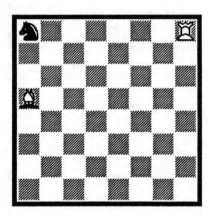

29 PROMOTION

The pawn's ability to advance and promote upon reaching the last row is a vital tactical weapon. Usually, one promotes to a new queen because an extra queen is almost always decisive. But there are times when less force is better and it is more effective to underpromote to a rook, bishop, or knight. For example, in a winning game you shouldn't promote to a queen if doing so stalemates your opponent. In such cases, it is better to delay promotion or to underpromote to a rook, for an extra rook is almost always a winning force. In other instances, you might prefer underpromoting to a knight because a knight can do what the queen can't: it can give a checking knight fork or a knight checkmate. Most of the time, however, direct promotion to a queen wins. In the accompanying diagrams, White's pawn advances to the last rank and promotes to a queen, giving checkmate.

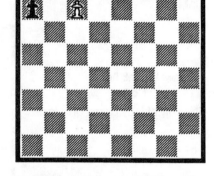

POSITION: **W: Pc7**
     B: Ka8 Pa7
It's White's turn.

POSITION: **W: Pc8**
     B: Ka8 Pa7
White has just advanced the pawn to the last rank, but has not completed the move.

POSITION: **W: Qc8**
     B: Ka8 Pa7
White has just promoted to a
queen, giving mate.

30 THE ANSWERS IN THIS BOOK

Let's go through a sample answer. For this discussion the
various parts are labeled a–g, but the actual problems are
not labeled at all.

TEST **41**   (a)

(Answers)
White to move   (b)

> **1** W: Kg6   Qh6   (c)   MATE   (d)
>   B: Kg8   (e)
>   1.   Qh6-g7 + +   (f)
> The queen mates, supported by the king.   (g)

(a)   TEST 41
       Indicates the test number. There are 30 tests, numbered 1–30.

(b)   White to move
       Indicates which player makes the winning move. Each test
       contains problems with only "White to move" or "Black to
       move."

(c)   1. W: Kg6 Qh6
This tells us the problem number and the placement of the
White units (Kg6 means there is a White king on g6; Qh6
means there is a White queen on h6). This lets us verify the
correctness of the original problem diagram and expedites
the learning of notation.

(d)   MATE
This is the name of the winning tactic. Other tactics are fork,
pin, skewer, discovery, undermining, overload, trapping, *en
prise*, x-ray, and promotion.

(e)   B: Kg8
This tells us the Black king is on g8.

(f)   1. Qh6-g7 + +
This means that White's winning move is "Queen on h6 moves
to g7, giving checkmate."

(g)   The queen mates, supported by the king.
This is an explanation of the winning move. Sometimes it
merely puts the notation into words; in other cases it explains
something additional about the winning move.

A FINAL WORD

That concludes our brief introduction to the game of chess
and its tactical weaponry. You are now ready to proceed to
the first test. Get a chessboard and pieces ready if you
wish, but all you should need is a pencil and paper to tally
your results. If you prefer, write your answers in the spaces
provided alongside each diagram and check the results
test by test. Every example is worth one point. Your pro-
gress can be charted in the table at the back of the book.
Try to complete each test in no more than thirty minutes.
That gives you an average of three minutes per problem.
Do a test every day and complete the course in a month.
Good luck.

THIRTY
TESTS

TEST **1**

White to move

Examples 1–10

SCORE   _____

CUMULATIVE SCORE   _____

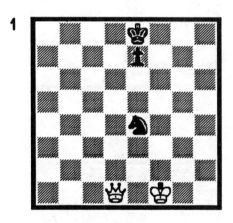

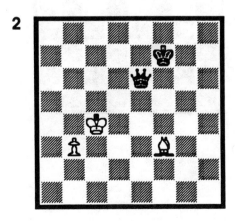

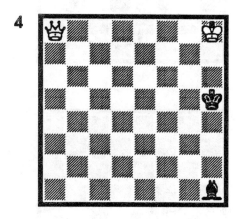

5

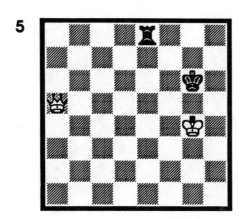

6

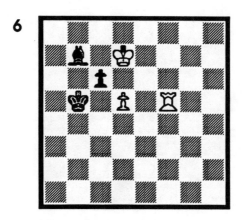

7

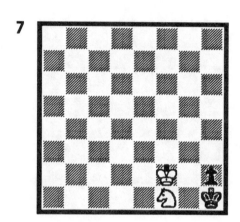

8

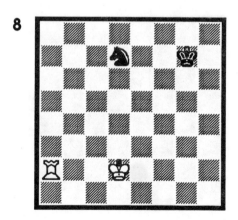

9

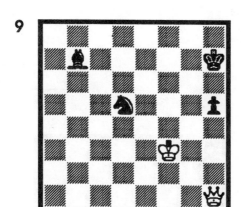

10

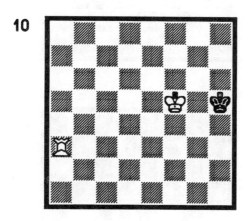

TEST 2

White to move

Examples 11–20

SCORE

CUMULATIVE SCORE

11

12

13

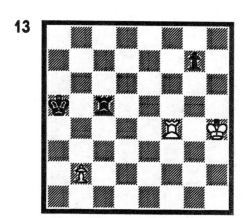

14

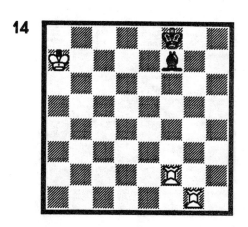

15

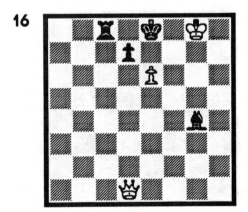

16

17

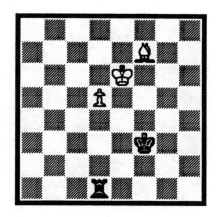

18

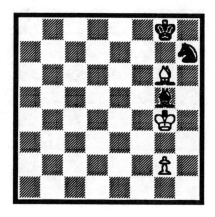

19

20

TEST **3**

White to move

Examples 21–30

SCORE

CUMULATIVE SCORE

21

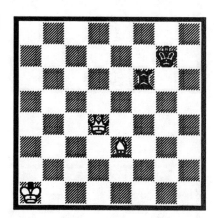

22

23

24

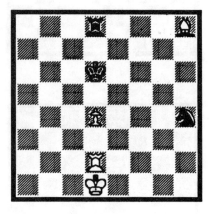

25

26

27

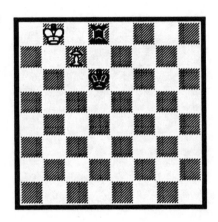

28

29

30

TEST **4**

White to move

Examples 31–40

SCORE _____

CUMULATIVE SCORE _____

31

32

33

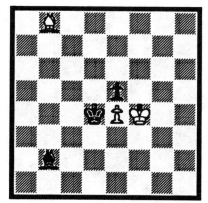

34

35

36

37

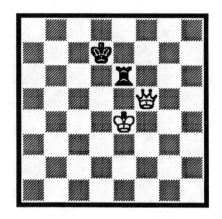

38

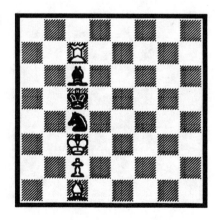

39

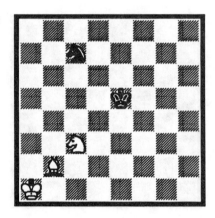

40

TEST **5**

White to move

Examples 41–50

SCORE

CUMULATIVE SCORE

41

42

43

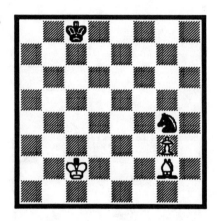

44

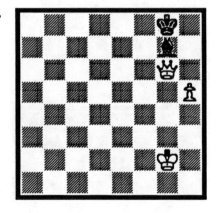

45

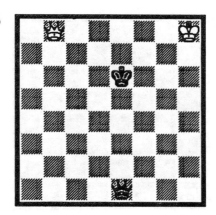

46

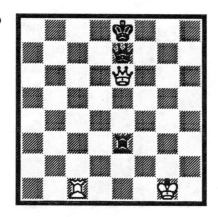

47

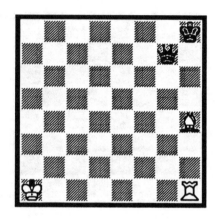

48

49

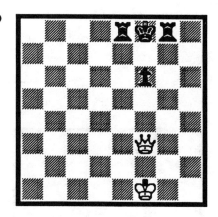

50

TEST **6**

White to move

Examples 51–60

SCORE _____

CUMULATIVE SCORE _____

53

54

55

56

57

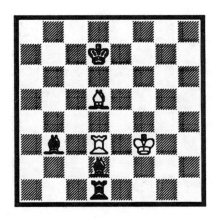

58

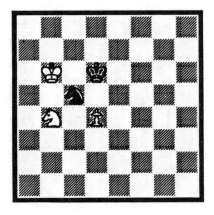

59

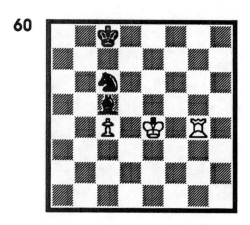

60

TEST 7

White to move

Examples 61–70

SCORE   _____

CUMULATIVE SCORE   _____

61

62

63

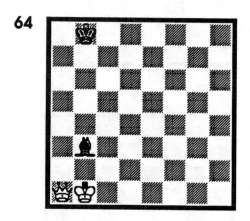

64

65

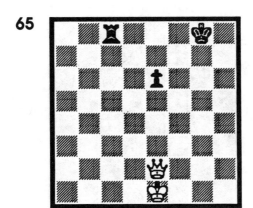

66

67

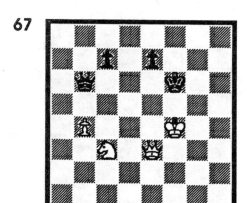

68

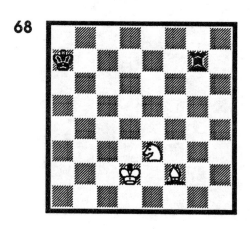

69

70

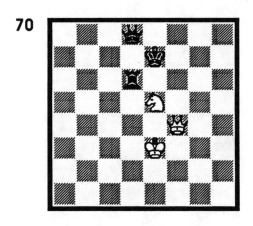

TEST **8**

White to move

Examples 71–80

SCORE _____

CUMULATIVE SCORE _____

71

72

73

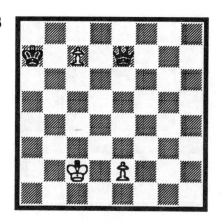

74

75

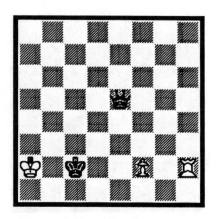

76

77

78

79

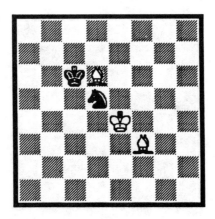

80

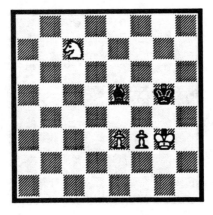

TEST **9**

White to move

Examples 81–90

SCORE

CUMULATIVE SCORE

81

82

83

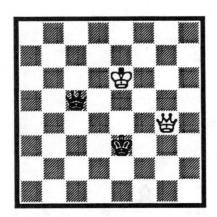

84

85

86

87

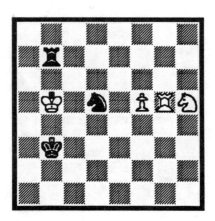

88

89

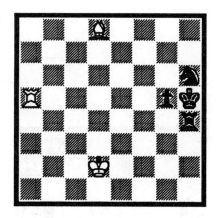

90

TEST **10**

White to move

Examples 91–100

SCORE _____

CUMULATIVE SCORE _____

91

92

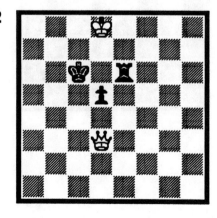

93

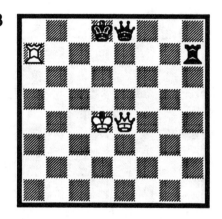

94

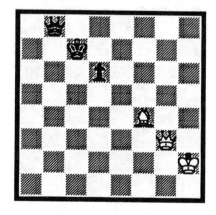

95

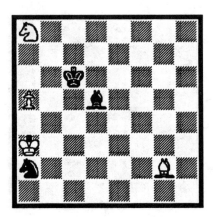

96

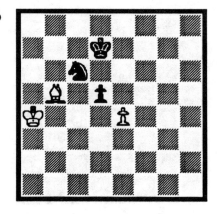

97

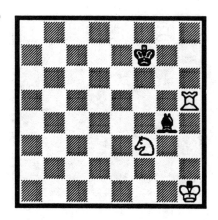

98

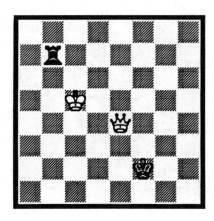

99

100

TEST **11**

Black to move

Examples 101–110

SCORE

CUMULATIVE SCORE

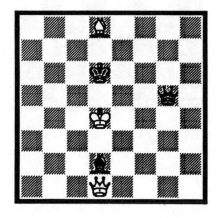

103

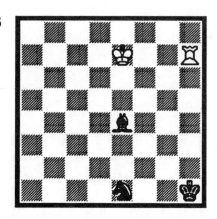

104

105

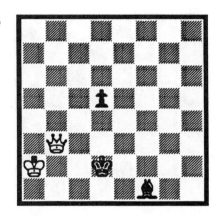

106

107

108

109

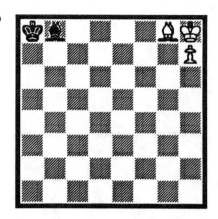

110

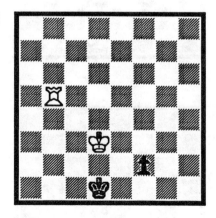

TEST **12**

Black to move

Examples 111–120

SCORE

CUMULATIVE SCORE

111

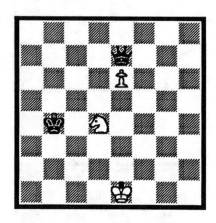

112

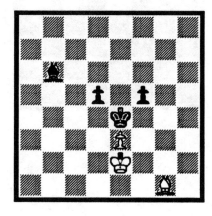

113

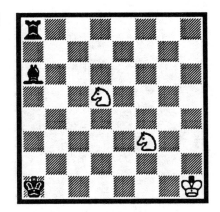

114

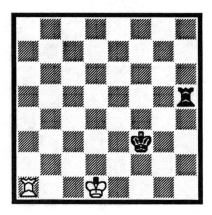

115

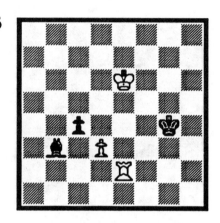

116

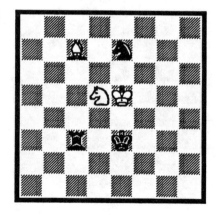

117

118

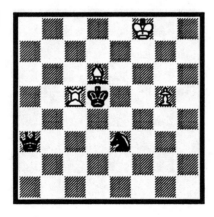

119

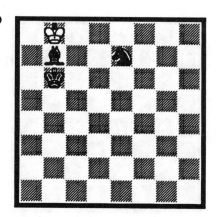

120

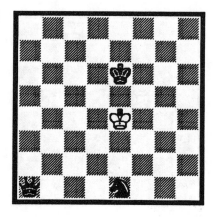

TEST **13**

Black to move

Examples 121–130

SCORE _____

CUMULATIVE SCORE _____

121

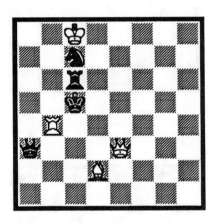

122

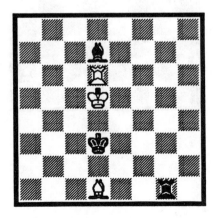

123

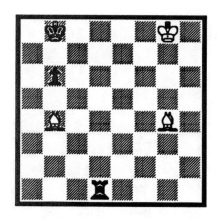

124

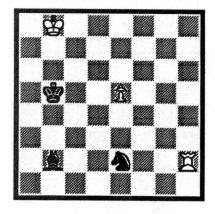

125

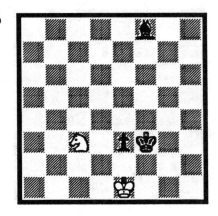

126

127

128

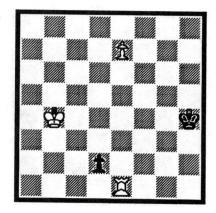

129

130

TEST **14**

Black to move

Examples 131–140

SCORE

CUMULATIVE SCORE

131

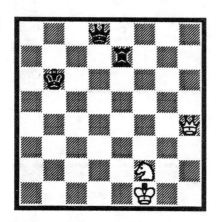

132

133

134

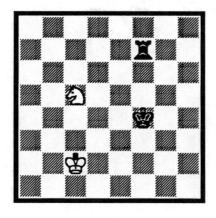

135

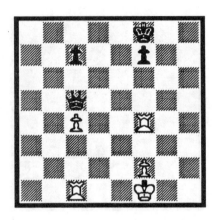

136

137

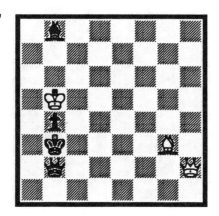

138

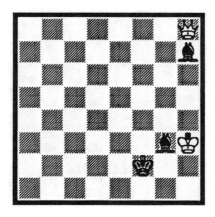

139

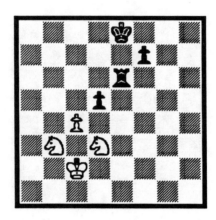

140

TEST **15**

Black to move

Examples 141–150

SCORE

CUMULATIVE SCORE

141

142

143

144

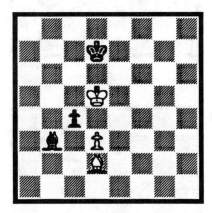

145

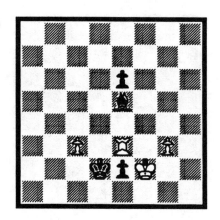

146

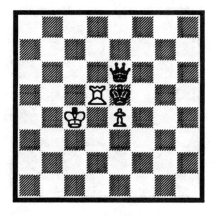

147

148

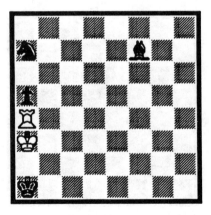

149

150

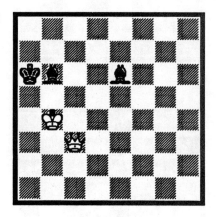

TEST **16**

Black to move

Examples 151–160

SCORE

CUMULATIVE SCORE

151

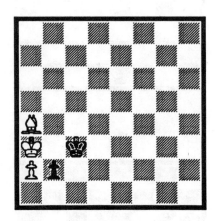

152

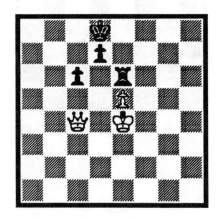

153

154

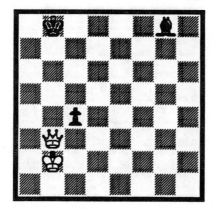

155

156

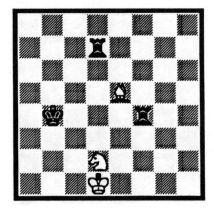

157

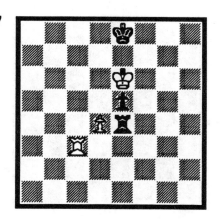

158

159

160

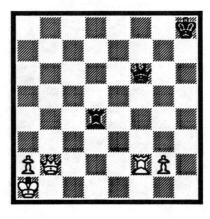

TEST **17**

Black to move

Examples 161–170

SCORE

CUMULATIVE SCORE

163

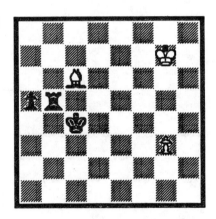

164

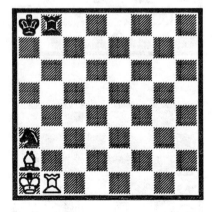

165

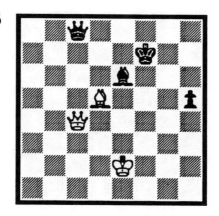

166

167

168

169

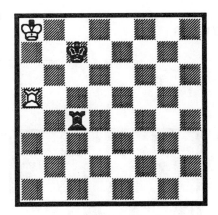

170

TEST **18**

Black to move

Examples 171–180

SCORE

CUMULATIVE SCORE

171

172

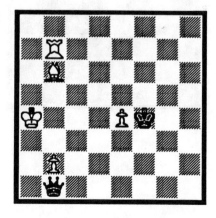

173

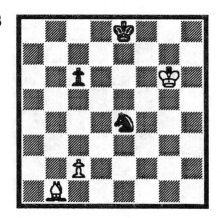

174

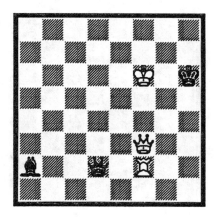

175

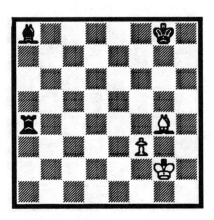

176

177

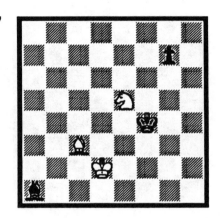

178

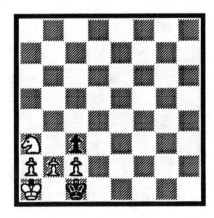

179

180

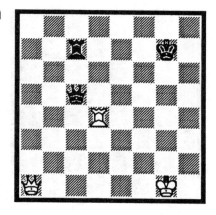

TEST **19**

Black to move

Examples 189–190

SCORE

CUMULATIVE SCORE

181

182

183

184

185

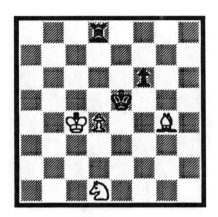

186

187

188

189

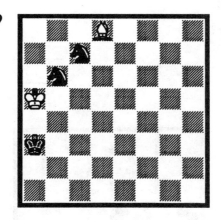

190

TEST **20**

Black to move

Examples 191–200

SCORE

CUMULATIVE SCORE

191

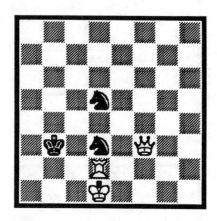

192

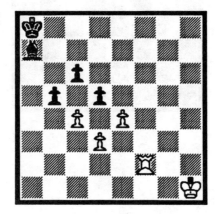

193

194

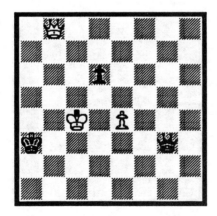

195

196

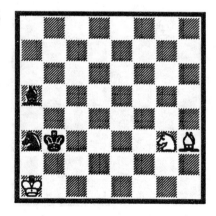

197

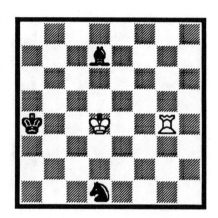

198

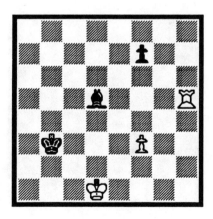

199

200

TEST **21**

White to move

Examples 201–210

SCORE _____

CUMULATIVE SCORE _____

201

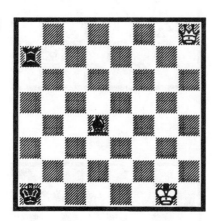

202

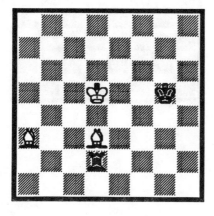

203

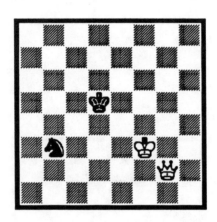

204

205

206

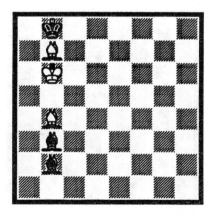

207

208

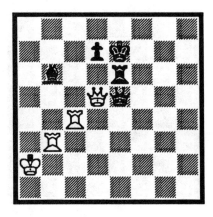

209

210

TEST **22**

White to move

Examples 211–220

SCORE _____

CUMULATIVE SCORE _____

211

212

213

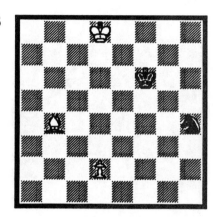

214

215

216

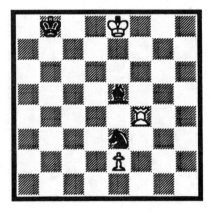

217

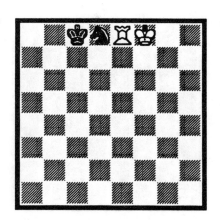

218

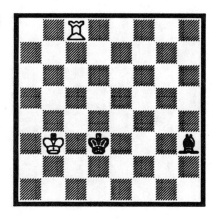

219

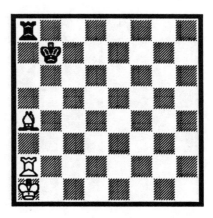

220

TEST **23**

White to move

Examples 221–230

SCORE _____

CUMULATIVE SCORE _____

221

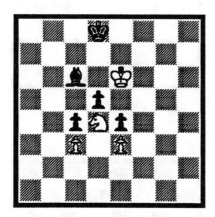

222

223

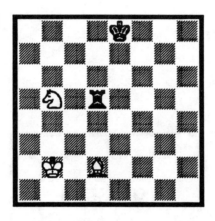

224

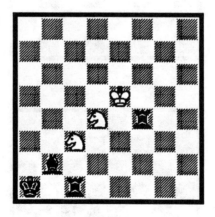

225

226

227

228

229

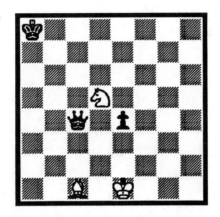

230

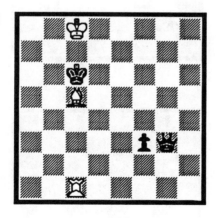

TEST **24**

White to move

Examples 231–240

SCORE

CUMULATIVE SCORE

231

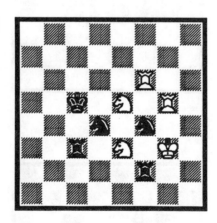

232

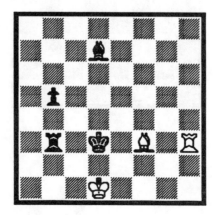

233

234

235

236

237

238

239

240

TEST **25**

White to move

Examples 241–250

SCORE _____

CUMULATIVE SCORE _____

241

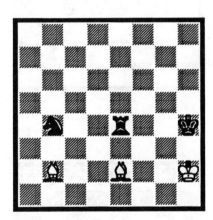

242

243

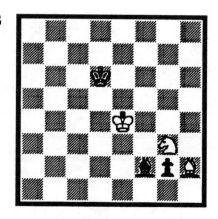

244

245

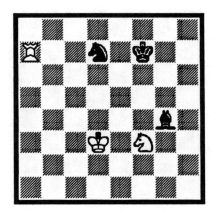

246

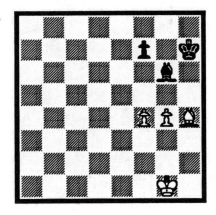

247

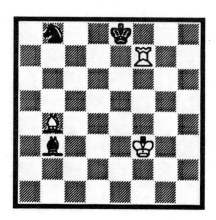

248

249

250

TEST **26**

Black to move

Examples 251–260

SCORE

CUMULATIVE SCORE

251

252

253

254

255

256

257

258

259

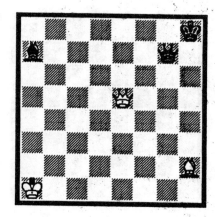

260

TEST **27**

Black to move

Examples 261–270

SCORE

CUMULATIVE SCORE

261

262

263

264

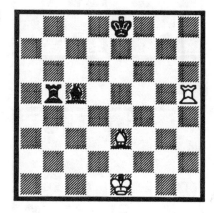

265

266

267

268

269

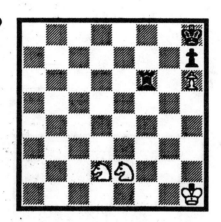

270

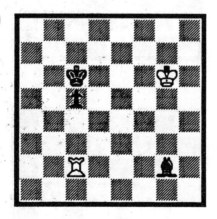

TEST **28**

Black to move

Examples 271–280

SCORE _____

CUMULATIVE SCORE _____

271

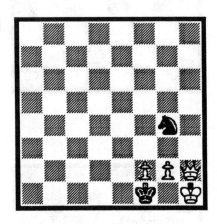

272

273

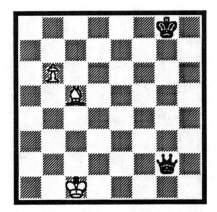

274

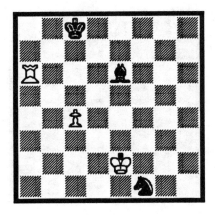

275

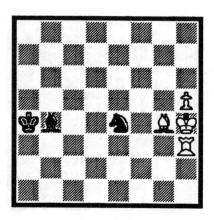

276

277

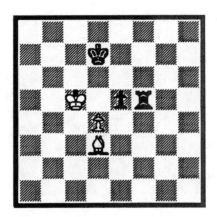

278

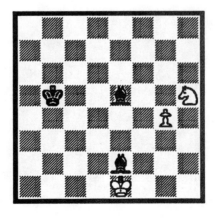

279

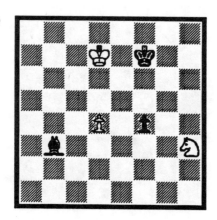

280

TEST **29**

Black to move

Examples 281–290

SCORE

CUMULATIVE SCORE

281

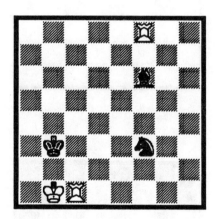

282

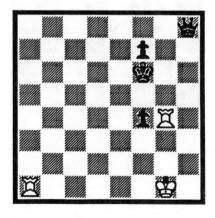

283

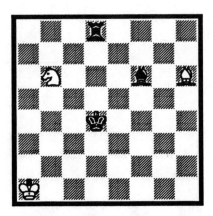

284

285

286

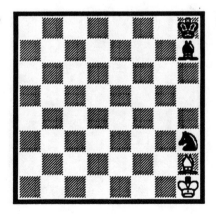

287

288

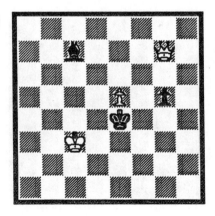

289

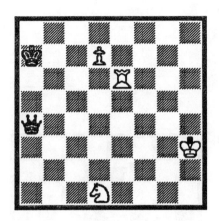

290

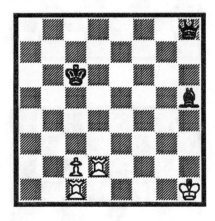

TEST **30**

Black to move

Examples 291–300

SCORE _____

CUMULATIVE SCORE _____

291

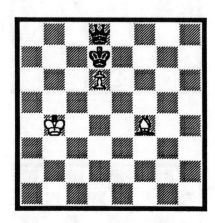

292

293

294

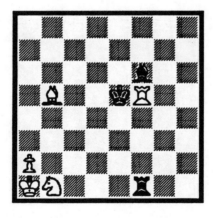

295

296

297

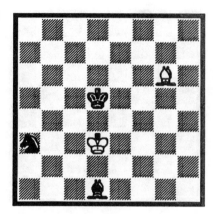

298

299

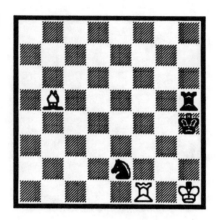

300

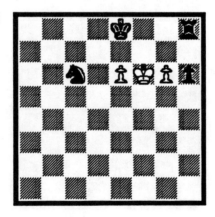

ANSWERS

APPENDICES

TEST 1

(Answers 1–10)
White to move

1 W: Kf1   Qd1   FORK
    B: Ke8   Ne4   Pe7
    1.   Qd1–a4+
The queen forks the king and knight. Next move, the queen takes the knight for nothing.

2 W: Kc4   Bf3   Pb3   PIN
    B: Kf7   Qe6
    1.   Bf3–d5
White blocks the check with the bishop, pinning the Black queen to the king. The queen is lost for the bishop. White wins the endgame.

3 W: Kf7   Rh7   Na7   OVERLOAD
    B: Kd7   Be7   Nc6
    1.   Na7×c6
Black's king is overloaded. If it takes the knight, White takes the bishop, winding up a full rook ahead.

4 W: Kh8   Qa8   *EN PRISE*
    B: Kh5   Bh1
    1.   Qa8×h1+
The queen takes the bishop for nothing.

5 W: Kg4   Qa5   SKEWER
    B: Kg6   Re8
    1.   Qa5–h5+
The queen skewers the king and rook. Next move, the queen takes the rook for nothing.

6 W: Kd7   Rf5   Pd5   DISCOVERY
    B: Kb5   Bb7   Pc6
    1.   d5×c6+
The rook discovers a check. Next move, the pawn takes the bishop.

7 W: Kf2 Nf1 MATE
B: Kh1 Ph2
1. Nf1–g3++
The knight mates the king in the corner.

8 W: Kd2 Ra2 PIN
B: Kg7 Nd7
1. Ra2–a7
The rook pins the knight to the king. Next move, the rook takes the knight for nothing.

9 W: Kf3 Qh1 FORK
B: Kh7 Bb7 Nd5 Ph5
1. Qh1–b1+
The queen forks the king and bishop. Next move, the queen takes the bishop for nothing.

10 W: Kf5 Ra3 MATE
B: Kh5
1. Ra3–h3++
The rook mates the king along the edge.

TEST **2**

(Answers 11–20)

White to move

11 W: Kf3 Ra1 Ba8 MATE
B: Kh1 Ng1
1. Kf3–g3++
The bishop discovers mate. The knight can't block the check because it's pinned to Black's king by the rook.

12 W: Ke1 Qe8 Ne7 DISCOVERY
B: Ka5 Qe5 Be4
1. Ne7–c6+
White checks to gain time. After the bishop takes the knight, White's queen takes Black's.

13   W: Kh4   Rf4   Pb2   FORK
         B: Ka5   Rc5   Pg7
         1.   b2–b4+
The pawn forks the king and rook. Next move, the pawn takes the rook. Whoever moves first has the same shot.

14   W: Ka7   Rf2   Rg1   PIN
         B: Kf8   Bf7
         1.   Rg1–f1
White piles up on the pinned bishop by doubling rooks. Next move, White takes the bishop for nothing.

15   W: Kh1   Qg2   *EN PRISE*
         B: Ka8   Qc6
         1.   Qg2×c6+
White's queen takes Black's queen for good.

16   W: Kg8   Qd1   Pe6   MATE
         B: Ke8   Rc8   Bg4   Pd7
         1.   Qd1×d7++
White's queen, supported by the pawn, takes and mates.

17   W: Ke6   Bf7   Pd5   SKEWER
         B: Kf3   Rd1
         1.   Bf7–h5+
The bishop skewers the king and rook. Next move, the bishop takes the rook for nothing.

18   W: Kg4   Bg6   Pg2   UNDERMINING
         B: Kg8   Bg5   Nh7
         1.   Bg6×h7+
White takes the knight that protects the bishop, and gives check. Next move, the king takes the bishop.

19   W: Ke7   Re1   FORK
         B: Kg4   Bc4
         1.   Re1–e4+
The rook forks the bishop and king. Next move, the rook takes the bishop for nothing.

20 W: Kg3   Bc3   Nc7   PIN
       B: Kf6   Ne5
       1.   Kg3–f4
White piles on the pinned knight. Next move, White takes the knight for nothing.

TEST 3

(Answers 21–30)

White to move

21 W: Ka1   Qd4   Be3   PIN
       B: Kg7   Rf6
       1.   Be3–g5
White piles on the pinned rook. Next move, White takes the rook for nothing.

22 W: Kd6   Qg1   MATE
       B: Kd8   Qa1
       1.   Qg1–g8++
The queen mates. Taking Black's queen is the second best move.

23 W: Kd3   Qd1   Pd2   FORK
       B: Kd8   Rc5   Re5   Pd5
       1.   Kd3–d4
White's king forks both rooks and will win one of them.

24 W: Kd1   Rd2   Bh8   Pd4   FORK
       B: Kd6   Rd8   Nh4
       1.   Bh8–f6
The bishop forks the rook and knight. Next move, it takes one of them.

25 W: Ke4   Rc6   Bd5   DISCOVERY
       B: Kb7   Rh1   Ne1
       1.   Rc6–h6+
White's rook gets a free attack on Black's rook while it unveils a bishop check. Next move, White takes the rook for nothing.

26 W: Ke1   Ra1   *EN PRISE*
        B: Ke8   Ra8
        1.   Ra1 × a8 +
White's rook takes Black's for nothing. Whoever goes first wins the other player's rook.

27 W: Kb8   Pc7   PROMOTION
        B: Kd6   Rd8
        1.   c7 × d8(Q) +
The pawn takes the rook for nothing, promoting to a queen and giving check. Promoting to a rook would also win.

28 W: Kg8   Ra7   SKEWER
        B: Kg6   Qg1
        1.   Ra7–g7 +
The rook skewers the king and queen. Next move, it takes the queen for free.

29 W: Kh6   Ra7   MATE
        B: Kh8   Rg8   Pg6
        1.   Ra7–h7 + +
White's rook, supported by the pawn, mates.

30 W: Kg1   Qg5   Rd1   X-RAY
        B: Kg8   Qd8   Rd4   Pg7
        1.   Qg5 × d8 +
White's queen takes Black's. White's rook supports this capture through Black's rook. White ends up a rook ahead.

TEST 4

(Answers 31–40)

White to move

31 W: Kg2   Qg8   Rc4   DISCOVERY
        B: Ka2   Qa3   Ra4
        1.   Rc4 × a4 +
This is the best line. White discovers check, steals a rook, pins the queen, and takes it next move.

32   W: Kg2   Ba2   Pd2   FORK
     B: Kg8   Ra8   Bd5
     1.   Ba2 × d5 +
White gets out of check by taking the Black bishop, forking king and rook. Next move, White takes the rook.

33   W: Kf4   Bb8   Pe4   SKEWER
     B: Kd4   Bb2   Pe5
     1.   Bb8 × e5 +
White gets out of check by taking the pawn with the bishop, skewering king and bishop. Next move, White takes the bishop.

34   W: Kf2   Rd3   MATE
     B: Kh1   Rd1
     1.   Rd3–h3 + +
White's rook mates. Taking Black's rook instead doesn't win as quickly.

35   W: Kc8   Pb6   MATE
     B: Ka8   Ba7   Nc7
     1.   b6–b7 + +
A simple pawn mate.

36   W: Kb2   Rc2   Rd2   Be2   OVERLOAD
     B: Kb7   Rg7   Nd7   Bg4
     1.   Be2 × g4
Bishop takes bishop. Black's rook is overloaded, unable to defend both pieces. If the rook takes the bishop, Black's knight is lost.

37   W: Ke4   Qf5   PIN
     B: Kd7   Re6
     1.   Ke4–d5
White gets out of check by piling on the pinned rook. The queen takes the rook next move.

38   W: Kc3   Rc7   Bc1   Pc2   OVERLOAD
     B: Kc5   Bc6   Nc4
     1.   Rc7 × c6 +
Black can't defend both his pieces. White takes the bishop to get two pieces for one.

39 W: Ka1 Bb2 Nc3   DISCOVERY
B: Ke5 Nc7
1. Nc3–b5 +
White's knight attacks Black's while the bishop discovers check. Next move, White takes Black's knight.

40 W: Kf7 Bg3 Nf3   FORK
B: Kh7 Qh3
1. Nf3–g5 +
The knight forks king and queen, winning the queen.

TEST 5

(Answers 41–50)

White to move

41 W: Kc4 Nd5 Pb5   FORK
B: Ke8 Ra8
1. Nd5–c7 +
The knight forks king and rook. Next move, it takes the rook for free.

42 W: Kh1 Qd1   FORK
B: Kg8 Rc8
1. Qd1–g4 +
The queen forks king and rook. Then it takes the rook.

43 W: Kc2 Bg2 Pg3   PIN
B: Kc8 Ng4
1. Bg2–h3
The bishop pins the knight to the king. Next move, it takes the knight for nothing.

44 W: Kg2 Qg6 Ph5   PIN
B: Kg8 Bg7
1. h5–h6
The pawn piles on the pinned bishop, which is lost.

45 W: Kh8 Qb8   SKEWER
B: Ke6 Qe1
1. Qb8–e8 +
White's queen skewers king and queen. Next move, Black's queen is taken for free.

46 W: Kg1 Qe6 Rc1   MATE
    B: Ke8 Qe7 Re3
1.   Rc1–c8 + +
The rook mates. Black's queen is unable to block it because it is pinned.

47 W: Ka1 Rh1 Bh4   DISCOVERY
    B: Kh8 Qg7
1.   Bh4–f6 +
The bishop pins the queen, uncovering the rook's check. The queen is lost.

48 W: Kd5 Bf3 Pe4   *EN PRISE*
    B: Ka8 Nh1
1.   Bf3 × h1
The bishop takes the knight for nothing.

49 W: Kf1 Qf3   MATE
    B: Kf8 Re8 Rg8 Pf6
1.   Qf3 × f6 + +
The queen takes the pawn, mating.

50 W: Kc6 Re4 Ne6   MATE
    B: Kh6 Re8 Rg6
1.   Re4–h4 + +
The rook mates. The knight thwarts escape.

TEST 6

(Answers 51–60)
White to move

51 W: Ka5 Qe5 Rc5   MATE
    B: Kc8 Qc7 Rc1
1.   Qe5 × c7 + +
Queen, supported by rook, takes queen, gives mate.

52 W: Kf5 Qg5   SKEWER
    B: Kd5 Qd1
1.   Qg5–d8 +
White's queen skewers king and queen. Next move, it takes the opposing queen for nothing.

53 W: Kf1 Rd1   PIN
      B: Ke8 Ne4
      1. Rd1–e1
The rook pins and wins the knight.

54 W: Kb1 Bh1 Pe3   FORK
      B: Kh7 Nb7 Pe4
      1. Bg2 × e4 +
The bishop forks king and knight. Next move, bishop takes knight for nothing.

55 W: Ke6 Rc7 Rd7   MATE
      B: Ke8 Rf7 Rg7
      1. Rc7–c8 + +
The rook on the left mates.

56 W: Ke1 Pd5 Pe5 Pf5   FORK
      B: Kd7 Rf7
      1. e5–e6 +
The middle pawn forks king and rook. Next move, the pawn takes the rook and White wins the ending.

57 W: Kf3 Rd3 Bd5   DISCOVERY
      B: Kd7 Rd1 Bb3 Bd2
      1. Bd5 × b3 +
White's bishop takes Black's, unveiling a rook check. Black's rook is plundered.

58 W: Kb6 Nb4 Pd4   *EN PRISE*
      B: Kd6 Nc5
      1. d4 × c5 +
The pawn, supported by White's king, takes the knight.

59 W: Ka1 Rh8   SKEWER
      B: Kf1 Nc1
      1. Rh8–h1 +
The rook skewers king and knight. The rook then takes the knight.

60 W: Ke4 Rg4 Pc4   FORK
      B: Kc8 Bc5 Nc6
      1. Ke4–d5
The king forks bishop and knight. One of them dies.

TEST 7

(Answers 61–70)

White to move

61 W: Kh1 Qa1   SKEWER
    B: Kh6 Bh3
    1. Qa1–h8 +

The queen skewers king and bishop. Next move, the queen takes the bishop for nothing.

62 W: Kb3 Qh8   MATE
    B: Kb1 Qa8
    1. Qh8–b2 + +

White's queen, supported by the king, gives mate. This is better than taking Black's queen.

63 W: Kd1 Qd8 Ra4   X-RAY
    B: Kd3 Qh4 Rd4
    1. Qd8 × h4

White's queen takes Black's, with x-ray support from White's rook. White wins at least a rook.

64 W: Kb1 Qa1   PIN
    B: Kb8 Bb3
    1. Qa1–b2

The queen pins the bishop, than takes it.

65 W: Ke1 Qe2   FORK
    B: Kg8 Rc8 Pe6
    1. Qe2 × e6 +

The queen takes the pawn, forking king and rook, winning the rook.

66 W: Kb4 Qd5 Rc5   *EN PRISE*
    B: Kf5 Qe5 Rg6
    1. Qd5 × e5 +

With rook support, White takes Black's queen.

67 W: Kf4   Qe3   Nc3   Pb4   FORK
     B: Kf6   Qb6   Pc7   Pe7
     1.   Nc3–d5 +
The knight forks all four of Black's units. After Black saves the king, White takes the queen.

68 W: Kd2   Ne3   Bf2   DISCOVERY
     B: Ka7   Rg7
     1.   Ne3–f5 +
The knight moves, unmasking a check from the bishop. The rook is then expropriated.

69 W: Kg2   Rc2   Bg6   OVERLOAD
     B: Kc6   Re4   Nc4   Pd5
     1.   Bg6 × e4
The bishop takes the rook. Black's pawn is overloaded, unable to take the bishop without abandoning the knight to White's rook.

70 W: Ke3   Qf4   Ne5   MATE
     B: Ke7   Qd8   Rd6
     1.   Qf4–f7 ++
The knight supports the queen's mate.

TEST 8

(Asnwers 71–80)

White to move

71 W: Kd1   Bh5   Pb3   SKEWER
     B: Kd5   Qb7   Pf3
     1.   Bh5 × f3 +
The bishop takes the pawn and skewers king and queen. Next move, it takes the queen for free.

72 W: Kd1   Qc1   Nf6   MATE
     B: Kh8   Qf1   Ne1
     1.   Qc1–h6 ++
The queen enters diagonally and mates.

73   W: Kc2   Pc7   Pe2   PROMOTION
        B: Ka7   Qe7
        1.   c7–c8(N)+
White promotes to a knight, forking king and queen, filching queen.

74   W: Kh1   Rb1   FORK
        B: Kh7   Nb8   Pb7
        1.   Rb1 × b7+
The rook takes the pawn, forking king and knight. Next move, the rook takes the knight for nothing.

75   W: Ka2   Rh2   Pf2   DISCOVERY
        B: Kc2   Qe5
        1.   f2–f4+
The pawn gets a free attack on the queen by unblocking a check from the rook. The pawn gets the queen.

76   W: Kc2   Qc4   Pe2   PIN
        B: Ke6   Nd5   Pc6
        1.   e2–e4
White piles on the pinned knight, pilfering the knight. This is better than taking the pawn with check.

77   W: Kh5   Bh1   Pb2   TRAPPING
        B: Kh8   Na5
        1.   Bh1–d5
The bishop repositions, corralling the knight. The pawn then advances two squares and the knight is lost.

78   W: Kc5   Qe6   MATE
        B: Ka4   Qa6
        1.   Qe6–a2++
The queen gives instant mate. This is better than instant win of the queen.

79   W: Ke4   Bf3   Bd6   PIN
        B: Kc6   Nd5
        1.   Ke4–e5
The king moves, revealing a pin. The knight falls.

80 W: Kg3   Nc7   Pe3   Pf3   FORK
     B: Kg5   Be5
     1.   f3–f4 +
The pawn forks king and bishop, then captures the bishop.

TEST 9

(Answers 81–90)

White to move

81 W: Ka8   Bc6   Nd5   DISCOVERY
     B: Kh1   Qb1
     1.   Nd5–c3 +
The knight attacks the queen, uncovering a bishop check.
The queen is dead. Long live the knight.

82 W: Kf1   Nf6   Nf4   MATE
     B: Kf8   Nf7   Ng7
     1.   Nf4–g6 + +
A box of knights and it's mate.

83 W: Ke6   Qg4   SKEWER
     B: Ke3   Qc5
     1.   Qg4–g1 +
The queen skewers king and queen. Black's queen is taken
next move.

84 W: Kf2   Ra7   Ra5   PIN
     B: Kg5   Rg4   Bf5   Pf4
     1.   Ra7–f7
White piles on the pinned bishop, which is lost.

85 W: Ke4   Qb5   FORK
     B: Kg6   Ne6
     1.   Qb5–f5 +
Forking king and knight, the queen wins the knight.

86 W: Ke4   Bd1   Bg1   Pg4   OVERLOAD
     B: Ke6   Nd4   Nf4   Pe5
     1.   Bg1 × d4
Bishop takes knight, and the Black pawn is unable to take
back without abandoning the other knight.

87   W: Kb5   Rg5   Nh5   Pf5   FORK
     B: Kb3   Rb7   Nd5
     1.   Kb5–c6
The king forks rook and knight. Black must lose one of them.

88   W: Ka7   Qd3   *EN PRISE*
     B: Kg7   Bd2   Nd4
     1.   Qd3 × d4 +
By taking the knight with check, White also gets to take the bishop on the next move.

89   W: Kd2   Ra5   Bd8   MATE
     B: Kh5   Rh4   Nh6   Pg5
     1.   Ra5 × g5 + +
Supported by the bishop, the rook takes the pawn.

90   W: Ke8   Rh7   PIN
     B: Ke1   Be4
     1.   Rh7–e7
The rook pins the bishop and wins it next move.

TEST 10

(Answers 91–100)

White to move

91   W: Kd6   Rh7   Nh5   FORK
     B: Kg8   Qg4
     1.   Nh5 – f6 +
The knight forks king and queen. After the king moves to safety, the queen is taken.

92   W: Kd8   Qd3   SKEWER
     B: Kc6   Re6   Pd6
     1.   Qd3 – a6 +
The queen skewers king and rook. After the king moves out of check, the queen takes the rook.

93 W: Kd4   Qe4   Ra7   MATE
      B: Kd8   Qe8   Rh7
      1.   Qe4 – a8 + +
The queen moves along the diagonal to the back row, giving mate, the fatest way to win.

94 W: Kh2   Qg3   Bf4   SKEWER
      B: Kc7   Qb8   Pd6
      1.   Bg3 × d6 +
Backed up by the queen, the bishop takes the pawn, skewering king and queen. Next move, the bishop takes the queen.

95 W: Ka3   Bg2   Na8   Pa5   UNDERMINING
      B: Kc6   Bd5   Na2
      1.   Bf3 × d5 +
The bishop takes the bishop with check, removing the protector of Black's knight. Next move, take the knight.

96 W: Ka4   Bb5   Pe4   PIN
      B: Kd7   Nc6   Pd5
      1.   e4 × d5
The pawn takes the pawn, piling on and winning the pinned knight.

97 W: Kh1   Rh5   Nf3   FORK
      B: Kf7   Bg4
      1.   Nf3 – e5 +
The knight forks king and bishop. After the king moves to safety, the knight takes the bishop.

98 W: Kc5   Qe4   *EN PRISE*
      B: Kf2   Rb7
      1.   Qe4 × b7
The queen takes the rook.

99 W: Ke8   Rb8   Rh8   MATE
      B: Ka3   Ra2   Ra4
      1.   Rh8 – h3 + +
The corner rook mates.

100 W: Kb4 Rg6 Bb1   DISCOVERY
     B: Kh7 Qb7
     1.   Rg6 − b6 +
The rook blocks the queen check, uncovering the bishop
check. The queen is old news.

TEST 11

(Answers 101–110)

Black to move

101 W: Ka7 Pg7   *EN PRISE*
     B: Kg1 Ba1 Bd1
     1.   ...   Ba1 × g7
The bishop takes the pawn, preventing promotion.

102 W: Kd4 Qd1 Bd8   MATE
     B: Kd6 Qg5 Bd2
     1.   ...   Qg5 − d5 + +
The queen splits the kings, mating.

103 W: Ke7 Rh7   *EN PRISE*
     B: Kh1 Be4 Ne1
     1.   ...   Be4 × h7
Black gets out of check by taking the rook.

104 W: Kg1 Ba1 Na3 Pg3   FORK
     B: Kd3 Qd7
     1.   ...   Qd7 − a7 +
The queen forks the king and knight. White loses a piece.

105 W: Ka2 Qb3   PIN
     B: Kd2 Bf1 Pd5
     1.   ...   Bf1 − c4
The bishop pins queen to king. The queen is lost.

106 W: Ka4 Qa8   SKEWER
     B: Kb6 Rb2
     1.   ...   Rb2 − a2 +
The rook skewers king and queen. After the king moves out
of check, the rook takes the queen.

107 W: Kh5   Nd7   DISCOVERY
         B: Kf5   Rb5
         1.   . . .   Kf5 − e6 +
The king attacks the knight, uncovering a check from the rook. After White gets out of check, Black takes the knight.

108 W: Kc2   Bd2   Nb2   OVERLOAD
         B: Ka2   Re2   Pc7
         1.   . . .   Re2 × d2 +
Black exploits White's overloaded king by taking the bishop with the rook. When the king takes back, it abandons the knight.

109 W: Kh8   Bg8   Ph7   MATE
         B: Ka8   Bb8
         1.   . . .   Bb8 − e5 + +
A diagonal mate.

110 W: Kd3   Rb5   SKEWER
         B: Kd1   Pf2
         1.   . . .   f2 − f1(Q) +
The pawn advances to the last row, becoming a queen. The new queen gives check, skewering White's king and rook.

TEST **12**

(Answers 111–120)
Black to move

111 W: Ke1   Nd4   Pe6   FORK
         B: Kb4   Qe7
         1.   . . .   Qe7 − h4 +
The queen forks White's king and knight, winning the knight.

112 W: Ke2   Bg1   Pe3   PIN
         B: Ke4   Bb6   Pd5   Pf5
         1.   . . .   f5 − f4
The pawn attacks the pinned pawn, winning it next move.

113 W: Kh1 Nd5 Nf3   SKEWER
      B: Ka1 Ra8 Ba6
      1. ... Ba6 – b7
The bishop skewers the knights. No matter how White plays, a knight is lost.

114 W: Kd1 Ra1   SKEWER
      B: Kf3 Rh5
      1. ... Rh5 – h1 +
The rook checks along the rank, skewering king and rook. Next move: rook takes rook.

115 W: Ke6 Re2 Pd3   DISCOVERY
      B: Kg4 Bb3 Pc4
      1. ... c4 × d3 +
Black's pawn takes White's pawn, clearing the line for a discovered check. The rook is left to its fate.

116 W: Ke5 Bc7 Nd5   UNDERMINING
      B: Ke3 Rc3 Ne7
      1. ... Ne7 × d5
Black's knight takes White's, stopping its three-way fork and leaving the bishop unguarded. White loses a piece.

117 W: Kf4 Qd4 Rb4   X-RAY
      B: Kh4 Qd8 Ra4
      1. ... Qd8 × d4 +
Queen takes queen with x-ray support: rook through rook. Black winds up at least a rook ahead.

118 W: Kf8 Rc5 Bd6 Pg5   UNDERMINING
      B: Kd5 Qa3 Ne3
      1. ... Kd5 × d6
The king takes the bishop, removing the rook's support. The rook is lost. Check it out.

119 W: Kb8   MATE
      B: Kb6 Bb7 Ne7
      1. ... Ne7 – c6 + +
The knight completes a basic mating pattern.

120   W: Ke4   MATE
          B: Ke6   Qa1   Ne1
          1.   ...   Qa1−e5++
The queen gives the mate. The knight locks the door.

TEST **13**

(Answers 121–130)

Black to move

121   W: Kc8   Qe3   Rb4   Bd2   OVERLOAD
          B: Kc5   Qa3   Rc6   Nc7
          1.   ...   Qa3×e3
Queen takes queen. The bishop is overworked. Black comes
out at least a rook ahead.

122   W: Kd5   Rd6   Bd1   MATE
          B: Kd3   Rg1   Bd7
          1.   ...   Rg1−g5++
The rook mates. Black's bishop stands sentinel.

123   W: Kg8   Bb4   Bg4   FORK
          B: Kb8   Rd1   Pb6
          1.   ...   Rd1−d4
The rook forks the bishops. One of them is history.

124   W: Kb8   Rh2   Pe5   FORK
          B: Kb5   Bb2   Ne2
          1.   ...   Bb2×e5+
Bishop takes, forks, wins rook.

125   W: Ke1   Nc3   PIN
          B: Kf3   Bf8   Pe3
          1.   ...   Bf8−b4
The bishop pins the knight. White can't defend it.

126   W: Kc2   Qg2   Re1   SKEWER
          B: Kd7   Qf7   Pe7
          1.   ...   Qf7−a2+
The queen skewers king and queen. White's queen is fodder.

127 W: Kg1 Be3   DISCOVERY
       B: Kg3 Rg8
       1.   ...   Kg3 – f3 +
The king attacks the bishop, uncovering a rook check. The bishop is lost.

128 W: Kb4 Re1 Pe7   PROMOTION
       B: Kh4 Pd2
       1.   ...   d2 × e1(Q) +
The pawn takes the rook, promoting to a queen. After White gets out of check, White's last pawn is lost.

129 W: Kh1   MATE
       B: Kh3 Bd3 Be3
       1.   ...   Bd3 – e4 + +
The light-square bishop mates.

130 W: Kh5 Be2 Nb5   PIN
       B: Kh8 Qa5 Na8
       1.   ...   Na8 – c7
Black's knight piles on White's pinned knight. It falls next move.

TEST 14

(Answers 131–140)

Black to move

131 W: Kf1 Qh4 Nf2   DISCOVERY
       B: Kb6 Qd8 Re7
       1.   ...   Re7 – e1 +
The rook checks, unmasking an attack to White's queen, which is lost.

132 W: Kh4 Bc5 Nb3 Nd4   OVERLOAD
       B: Kc4 Rc8 Nc6 Pc7
       1.   ...   Nc6 × d4
The knight at b3 is overloaded. If it responds to the capture of the d4-knight it abandons the bishop. And if the bishop takes on d4, then White's knight on b3 is lost.

133 W: Kh2   Nd2   FORK
B: Ke5   Rf3
1.   . . .   Rf3 – f2 +
The rook forks king and knight.

134 W: Kc2   Nc5   PIN
B: Kf4   Rf7
1.   . . .   Rf7 – c7
The rook pins the knight and takes it next move.

135 W: Kf1   Rc1   Rf4   Pc4   Pf2   SKEWER
B: Kf8   Qc5   Pf7   Pc7
1.   . . .   Qc5 – g5
The queen skewers the rooks. If White moves either rook to
safety, it leaves the other one hanging.

136 W: Kh1   Nd3   Nf1   FORK
B: Kf3   Qa8
1.   . . .   Kf3 – e2 +
The king forks the two knights and the queen discovers
check. White loses a knight.

137 W: Kb5   Qh2   Bg3   X-RAY
B: Kb3   Qb2   Bb8   Pb4
1.   . . .   Qb2 × h2
Black's queen takes White's, with x-ray support from Black's
bishop through White's bishop. After White takes back the
queen, Black gains a bishop.

138 W: Kh3   Qh8   MATE
B: Kf2   Bg3   Bh7
1.   . . .   Bh7 – f5 + +
The light-square bishop delivers mate.

139 W: Kc2   Nb3   Nd3   Pc4   FORK
B: Ke8   Re6   Pd5   Pf7
1.   . . .   d5 × c4
The center pawn takes White's pawn, forking the knights
and winning one of them.

140   W: Ke1   Qd1   Bf1   Ne2   MATE
            B: Ke8   Ne4   Pf3
            1.   ...   f3 − f2 + +
The pawn mates. The knight supports.

TEST 15

(Answers 141–150)

Black to move

141   W: Kh8   Ra1   FORK
            B: Kg2   Qb7
            1.   ...   Qb7 − b2 +
The queen forks king and rook and takes the rook next move.

142   W: Kf5   Ne4   PIN
            B: Kg2   Bc2   Pd7
            1.   ...   d7 − d5
Black piles on the pinned knight with a two-square pawn move. Next move, the knight is taken for nothing.

143   W: Kf4   Qh6   Pd2   SKEWER
            B: Kc1   Qd8
            1.   ...   Qd8 × d2 +
The queen takes the pawn, checking and skewering king and queen. White's queen goes next.

144   W: Kd5   Bd2   Pd3   DISCOVERY
            B: Kd7   Bb3   Pc4
            1.   ...   c4 − c3 +
The pawn attacks the bishop, uncovering a bishop check. The pawn then captures the bishop.

145   W: Kf2   Re3   Pc3   Pg3   OVERLOAD
            B: Kd2   Be5   Pe2   Pe6
            1.   ...   Be5 × g3 +
The bishop takes the pawn, check. White's king and rook are overloaded. If the rook takes the bishop, Black promotes the pawn to a new queen with check. If the king takes the bishop, Black's king takes the rook and then promotes.

146   W: Kc4   Rd5   Pe4   UNDERMINING
          B: Ke5   Qe6
          1.   ...   Ke5 × e4
Black gets out of check by taking the pawn with the king,
undermining the rook's support. The rook is lost.

147   W: Kd4   Qg1   Na7   MATE
          B: Kb6   Qf8   Nf2
          1.   ...   Qf8 − c5 + +
The queen mates. Black's knight prevents escape.

148   W: Ka3   Ra4   MATE
          B: Ka1   Bf7   Na7   Pa5
          1.   ...   Na7 − b5 + +
The knight moves up and mates.

149   W: Ke3   Bg8   Ne7   FORK
          B: Kd1   Rf5   Bb2
          1.   ...   Rf5 − e5 +
The rook forks king and knight, winning the knight.

150   W: Kb4   Qc3   SKEWER
          B: Ka6   Bb6   Be6
          1.   ...   Bb6 − a5 +
The dark-square bishop skewers king and queen. The king
must move away from the queen, and the queen is lost.

TEST **16**

(Answers 151–160)

Black to move

151   W: Ka3   Ba4   Pa2   PROMOTION
          B: Kc3   Pb2
          1.   ...   b2 − b1(N) + +
The pawn advances and promotes to a knight. Checkmate.

152 W: Ke4 Qc4 Pe5 FORK
B: Kd8 Re6 Pc6 Pd7
1. . . . d7–d5 +
The pawn goes two squares, forking king and queen and winning the queen. The pinned e-pawn can't take it.

153 W: Kc3 Qb2 Pc2 SKEWER
B: Kc6 Bc7 Nc5
1. . . . Bc7–e5 +
The bishop skewers king and queen, wins the queen.

154 W: Kb2 Qb3 *EN PRISE*
B: Kb8 Bg8 Pc4
1. . . . c4 × b3
Black gets out of check by simply taking the queen.

155 W: Kh1 Qd3 Be3 Ph2 MATE
B: Kf1 Bd5 Pe4
1. . . . e4 × d3 + +
Black turns the tables by taking the queen with the pawn, uncovering a mating check from the bishop.

156 W: Kd1 Be5 Nd2 PIN
B: Kb4 Rd7 Rf4
1. . . . Rf4–f2
The attacked rook piles on the pinned knight. White loses a piece.

157 W: Ke6 Rc3 Pd4 DISCOVERY
B: Ke8 Re4 Pe5
1. . . . e5 × d4 +
The pawn takes the pawn, attacking White's rook and discovering check. Next move, the pawn takes White's rook and soon promotes.

158 W: Kc3 Bd4 Pd3 FORK
B: Ke6 Nd6 Pd5
1. . . . Nd6–b5 +
The knight forks king and bishop. The bishop is lost.

159   W: Kb6   Qd3   DISCOVERY
     B: Kb2   Qf2   Pc5
     1.   . . .   c5–c4 +
The pawn advances, attacking the queen and uncovering
check. White's queen is lost.

160   W: Ka1   Qb2   Rf2   Pa2   Pg2   MATE
     B: Kh8   Qf6   Rd4
     1.   . . .   Rd4–d1 + +
The rook mates. White's queen is pinned and can't help.

TEST 17

(Answers 161–170)

Black to move

161   W: Kd3   Bd1   Nd4   PIN
     B: Kb8   Rd8   Nf8
     1.   . . .   Nf8–e6
Black's knight piles on White's pinned knight, which is lost.

162   W: Kh2   Rh7   Bc2   Na4   OVERLOAD
     B: Kh4   Ra7   Ra6   Bh6
     1.   . . .   Ra7 × h7
Black trades rooks to exploit White's overloaded bishop.
The knight falls.

163   W: Kg7   Bc6   Pg3   FORK
     B: Kc4   Rb5   Pa5
     1.   . . .   Rb5–g5 +
The rook forks king and pawn, winning the pawn.

164   W: Ka1   Rb1   Ba2   MATE
     B: Ka8   Rb8   Na3
     1.   . . .   Na3–c2 + +
The knight mates.

165   W: Ke2   Qc4   Bd5   X-RAY
     B: Kf7   Qc8   Be6   Ph5
     1.   . . .   Qc8 × c4 +
Black's queen takes White's. White loses the bishop.

166   W: Kg1   Rb8   Bf1   Bh2   Pg2   MATE
      B: Kg8   Rb1   Rf8
      1.   ...   Rb1 × f1 + +
The rook on the back row takes the bishop, giving mate.

167   W: Ka2   Rg1   Na7   Pd4   Pg2   FORK
      B: Kd2   Rg4   Bg7   Pd7
      1.   ...   Bg7 × d4
The bishop takes the pawn, forking rook and knight. One of
the two must go.

168   W: Kc1   Bc6   PIN
      B: Ke3   Re8
      1.   ...   Re8–c8
The rook wins the bishop with a simple pin to the king.

169   W: Ka8   Ra5   DISCOVERY
      B: Kc7   Rc4
      1.   ...   Kc7–b6
The king attacks the rook and unveils a mate threat. To stop
mate, White must abandon the rook.

170   W: Kh1   Re4   FORK
      B: Kc6   Ng4   Pb7
      1.   ...   Ng4–f2 +
The knight forks king and rook, winning the rook.

TEST **18**

(Answers 171–180)

Black to move

171   W: Kb1   Qf3   FORK
      B: Kh7   Ne4   Pb7
      1.   ...   Ne4–d2 +
The knight forks king and queen. The queen is lost.

172   W: Ka4   Rb7   Bb6   Pb2   Pe4   FORK
      B: Kf4   Qb1
      1.   ...   Qb1 × e4 +
The queen forks king and rook and takes the rook next
move.

173 W: Kg6   Bb1   Pc2   TRAPPING
          B: Ke8   Ne4   Pc6
          1. . . .   Ne4–c3
The knight attacks and traps the bishop.

174 W: Kf6   Qf3   Rf2   MATE
          B: Kh6   Qd2   Ba2
          1. . . .   Qd2–g5++
The queen, supported by the king, mates.

175 W: Kg2   Bg4   Pf3   PIN
          B: Kg8   Ra4   Ba8
          1. . . .   Ra4×g4+
The rook takes the bishop, giving check. The pawn can't
take back because it's pinned to the king.

176 W: Kf3   Qd1   SKEWER
          B: Kf7   Bd7   Nf6
          1. . . .   Bd7–g4+
The bishop skewers king and queen, winning the queen.

177 W: Kd2   Bc3   Ne5   UNDERMINING
          B: Kf4   Ba1   Pg7
          1. . . .   Ba1×c3+
The bishop takes the bishop with check, removing its protection of the knight. The knight is lost.

178 W: Ka1   Na3   Pa2   Pb2   Pc2   MATE
          B: Kc1   Pc3
          1. . . .   c3×b2++
Pawn takes pawn—a pawn mate.

179 W: Ke4   Qe3   DISCOVERY
          B: Kg4   Re6   Be5
          1. . . .   Be5–f4+
The bishop attacks the queen, uncovering a check from the
rook. White loses the queen.

180 W: Kg1   Qa1   Rd4   PIN
          B: Kg7   Qc5   Rc7
          1. . . .   Rc7–d7
The Black rook attacks the pinned rook, which is lost.

TEST **19**

(Answers 181–190)
Black to move

181 W: Kh4 Bh1   DISCOVERY
     B: Kf2 Bb1 Be1
     1. ...   Kf2–g1 +
The king attacks the bishop, unveiling a bishop check. Next
move, Black takes the bishop in the corner.

182 W: Kh8 Rh1 Ng1 Ph2   TRAPPING
     B: Ka8 Ra1 Bf1
     1. ...   Bf1–g2
The bishop attacks the trapped rook and takes it next move.

183 W: Ke1 Rd1 Nd2   MATE
     B: Kd7 Bd3 Bd6
     1. ...   Bd6–g3 + +
The dark-square bishop mates.

184 W: Kb1 Qb3   PIN
     B: Kc6 Rd5 Pd7
     1. ...   Rd5–b5
The rook pins the queen. Black wins the endgame.

185 W: Kc4 Bg4 Nd1 Pd4   FORK
     B: Ke5 Rd8 Pf6
     1. ...   Rd8 × d4 +
The rook takes the pawn, forking White's pieces and winning one of them.

186 W: Kb1 Nf5 Nh3   SKEWER
     B: Kc8 Rd7 Bb3
     1. ...   Bb3–e6
The bishop skewers the knights. A knight is lost.

187 W: Kh7 Rd3 Nf5   FORK
     B: Kd5 Rd8 Pd7 Pe5
     1. ...   Kd5–e4
Black's king escapes check by splitting the rook and knight,
one of which must go.

188 W: Kd1 Qe3 Rf5   PIN
        B: Kc3 Qb5 Nd5
        1. . . .   Nd5×e3+

Black's knight gets out of the pin by taking the queen with check, winning easily.

189 W: Ka5 Bd8   MATE
        B: Ka3 Nb6 Nc7
        1. . . .   Nb6–c4++

The knight mates. Make sure you move the right one.

190 W: Kd2 Bd5 Nd4   SKEWER
        B: Kb2 Rb7 Pb4
        1. . . .   Rb7–d7

The rook skewers three pieces. White loses the bishop or the knight.

TEST **20**

(Answers 191–200)

Black to move

191 W: Kd1 Qf3 Rd2   MATE
        B: Kb3 Nd3 Nd5
        1. . . .   Nd5–c3++

The knight mates with a little help from its friends.

192 W: Kh1 Rf2 Pc4 Pd3 Pe3   *EN PRISE*
        B: Ka8 Ba7 Pb5 Pc6 Pd5
        1. . . .   Ba7×f2

Through a maze, the bishop takes the rook for nothing.

193 W: Ka2 Be2 Ne3   FORK
        B: Kg2 Re7 Pe6
        1. . . .   Kg2–f2

The king gets out of check by giving a fork. Either the knight or the bishop is lost.

194   W: Kc4   Qb8   Pe4   DISCOVERY
          B: Ka3   Qg3   Pd6
          1.   ...   d6–d5 +
The pawn checks, uncovering a winning attack to White's queen.

195   W: Kf6   Bc1   Bf1   SKEWER
          B: Kh1   Rb7   Bc6
          1.   ...   Rb7–b1
The rook skewers the bishops. White must lose one of them.

196   W: Ka1   Bh3   Ng3   MATE
          B: Kb3   Ba5   Na3
          1.   ...   Ba5–c3 + +
The bishop mates the cornered king.

197   W: Kd4   Rg4   *EN PRISE*
          B: Ka4   Bd7   Nd1
          1.   ...   Bd7 × g4
The bishop takes the rook for free.

198   W: Kd1   Rh5   Pf3   FORK
          B: Kb3   Bd5   Pf7
          1.   ...   Bd5 × f3 +
The bishop takes the pawn, forking king and rook. It takes the rook next move.

199   W: Kh1   Re5   Na1   Pe4   Pa4   SKEWER
          B: Ke7   Re8   Bh4   Pe6
          1.   ...   Bh4–f6
The bishop skewers rook and knight. White loses a piece.

200   W: Ka1   Qe1   MATE
          B: Ka5   Rb2   Nc3
          1.   ...   Rb2–a2 + +
The rook mates. The knight is a supportive partner.

TEST **21**

(Answers 201–210)
White to move

201 W: Kg1 Qh8   FORK
B: Ka1 Ra7 Bd4
1. Qh8 × d4 +
White gets out of check by taking the bishop, which forks king and rook. The rook goes next.

202 W: Kd5 Ba3 Bd3   PIN
B: Kg5 Rd2
1. Ba3–c1
The bishop pins and wins the rook.

203 W: Kf3 Qg2   SKEWER
B: Kd5 Nb3
1. Qg2–g8 +
The queen skewers king and knight and collects the knight next move.

204 W: Kd7 Pb3 Pf3   TRAPPING
B: Kf7 Nb7
1. b3–b4
The pawn advances, trapping the knight, which White's king will attack and win.

205 W: Kc6 Qe6 Bg6   MATE
B: Kf8 Qd8 Bb8
1. Qe6–f7 + +
The queen, supported by the bishop, gives mate.

206 W: Kb6 Bb7 Bb4   MATE
B: Kb8 Bb3 Bb2
1. Bb4–d6 + +
The dark-square bishop mates.

207 W: Ka4 Pb7   PROMOTION
B: Ka6 Pa5
1. b7–b8(R)
White avoids stalemate by promoting to a rook instead of to a queen, and wins easily.

208   W: Ka2   Qd5   Rb3   Rc4   OVERLOAD
         B: Ke7   Qe5   Re6   Bb6   Pd7
         1.   Qd5 × e5
White takes Black's queen, luring the rook out of position, and then wins the bishop.

209   W: Kh5   Qa5   Bb5   DISCOVERY
         B: Kd5   Qe6   Pf7
         1.   Bb5–d7 +
The bishop attacks the queen, uncovering check. Black loses the queen.

210   W: Kh8   Qh4   FORK
         B: Ke8   Ba8
         1.   Qh4–a4 +
The queen shifts to the other flank to fork king and bishop. The bishop is lost.

TEST 22

(Answers 211–220)

White to move

211   W: Kg5   Qd3   FORK
         B: Ke7   Ba5   Nc7
         1.   Qd3–a3 +
The queen forks king and bishop, capturing the bishop next move.

212   W: Kc7   Rc1   PIN
         B: Ka6   Na2
         1.   Rc1–a1
The rook pins the knight and takes it next move.

213   W: Kd8   Bb4   Pd2   SKEWER
         B: Kf6   Nh4
         1.   Bb4–e7 +
The bishop skewers king and knight, winning the knight.

214 W: Kf5   Nc6   Ne6   MATE
        B: Ka8   Nb7   Nd7
        1.   Ne6–c7 + +
The good knight mates.

215 W: Kf6   Qe7   FORK
        B: Kh4   Ra3   Ne1   Pb4
        1.   Qe7 × b4 +
It's better to take the pawn instead of the knight. Both go
with check, but capturing the pawn also wins the rook.

216 W: Ke8   Rf4   Pe2   FORK
        B: Kb8   Be5   Ne3
        1.   Rf4–e4
The rook forks bishop and knight. Black loses a piece.

217 W: Kf8   Re8   PIN
        B: Kc8   Nd8
        1.   Kf8–e7
The king piles on the pinned knight and next move the rook
takes it.

218 W: Kb3   Rc8   SKEWER
        B: Kd3   Bh3
        1.   Rc8–c3 +
The rook skewers king and bishop, gaining the bishop.

219 W: Ka1   Ra2   Ba4   DISCOVERY
        B: Kb7   Ra8
        1.   Ba4–c6 +
The bishop checks, uncovering an attack to the rook. Black's
rook can't be saved.

220 W: Ke4   Nh5   Nf3   MATE
        B: Kh1   Nd5   Ng2
        1.   Nh5–g3 + +
That's mate.

TEST 23

(Answers 221–230)

White to move

221 W: Ke6 Nd4 Pc3 Pe3   *EN PRISE*
     B: Kd8 Bc6 Pc4 Pd5 Pe4
     1.   Nd4 × c6 +
The knight takes the bishop for free.

222 W: Kg4 Qd1   FORK
     B: Kg8 Ne4
     1.   Qd1–d5 +
The queen forks king and knight, taking the knight next move.

223 W: Kb2 Bd2 Nb5   FORK
     B: Ke8 Rd5
     1.   Nb5–c7 +
The knight forks king and rook, winning the rook.

224 W: Ke5 Nc3 Nd4   MATE
     B: Ka1 Rc1 Rf4 Bb2
     1.   Nd4–b3 + +
The knight next to White's king mates.

225 W: Kc7 Rd7 Rg7   MATE
     B: Kf8 Rb8 Re8
     1.   Rd7–f7 + +
The rook next to White's king mates.

226 W: Kb1 Rh1 Bg1   PIN
     B: Kd1 Be1
     1.   Bg1–f2
The bishop attacks the bishop, unveiling the rook's pin. The bishop is lost.

227 W: Kc2 Qc1   SKEWER
     B: Kc6 Qa8
     1.   Qc1–h1 +
The queen skewers king and queen. After the king steps aside, Black's queen is taken.

228 W: Ka5 Qa1 Pd5   SKEWER
      B: Kd8 Bf8 Nf5 Pe5
      1.   Qa1–f1
The queen skewers knight and bishop, winning a piece.

229 W: Ke1 Bc1 Nd5   FORK
      B: Ka8 Qc4 Pe4
      1.   Nd5–b6+
The knight forks king and queen, winning the queen.

230 W: Kc8 Rc1 Bc5   DISCOVERY
      B: Kc6 Qg3 Pf3
      1.   Bc5–f2+
The bishop attacks the queen and the rook uncovers check. The queen goes down.

TEST 24

(Answers 231–240)

White to move

231 W: Kg3 Rf6 Rg5 Ne5 Ne3   MATE
      B: Kc5 Rc3 Rf2 Nd4 Nf4
      1.   Ne5–d3++
So many things to do, but this is the only instant mate.

232 W: Kd1 Rh3 Bf3   DISCOVERY
      B: Kd3 Rb3 Bd7 Pb5
      1.   Bf3–e2+
Both the bishop and rook check, and Black's rook is lost.

233 W: Ke5 Bb8 Pc3   DISCOVERY
      B: Kg3 Rg7
      1.   Ke5–f6+
The king attacks the rook, unveiling the bishop's discovered check. The rook is lost.

234 W: Ke4 Bb5 Ne3 Pc4 Pf5   FORK
      B: Kb6 Rc3 Bf6 Pc5 Pe5
      1.   Ne3–d5+
The knight forks Black's three pieces: king, rook, and bishop. White will take the rook.

235   W: Kd4   Rc4   Bb3   UNDERMINING
     B: Ke6   Bd5   Pc6
     1.   Rc4×c6+
The rook takes the pawn, removing the bishop's support.
The bishop falls.

236   W: Kc1   Qc2   Bb1   MATE
     B: Kg8   Qf8   Nf7
     1.   Qc2–h7++
The queen mates, supported by the bishop.

237   W: Kd1   Ra1   Rg1   Nb1   FORK
     B: Kd7   Rc4   Re4   Pd3   Pd4
     1.   Nb1–d2
The knight forks the rooks and White must win one of them.

238   W: Kg2   Rg7   SKEWER
     B: Kc5   Pc2
     1.   Rg7–c7+
The rook skewers king and pawn. King must move, pawn
goes.

239   W: Kf1   Rh1   Nf8   MATE
     B: Kh8   Qg8   Bg7   Ph7
     1.   Nf8–g6++
The knight mates because the pawn is pinned and can't
capture.

240   W: Ka3   Bf8   Nf3   TRAPPING
     B: Ka8   Nh8
     1.   Nf3–e5
The knight traps Black's knight. Next move, the bishop
attacks the cornered knight, and one move later wins it.

TEST **25**

(Answers 241–250)

White to move

241 W: Kh2   Bb2   Be2   MATE
       B: Kh4   Re4   Nb4
       1.   Bb2 – f6 + +

The dark-square bishop mates.

242 W: Ka4   Rh8   Bh6   MATE
       B: Kh4   Rg4
       1.   Bh6 – f4 + +

The bishop moves, but the rook mates. The bishop blocks the check and guards the escape squares.

243 W: Ke4   Bh2   Ng3   DISCOVERY
       B: Kd6   Bf2   Pg2
       1.   Ng3 – h1 +

The knight attacks the bishop, uncovering check. The bishop is lost.

244 W: Ka2   Qh3   FORK
       B: Kg8   Ba6   Pe6
       1.   Qh3 × e6 +

The queen takes the pawn with check, forking king and bishop, and collecting the bishop next move.

245 W: Kd3   Ra7   Nf3   FORK
       B: Kf7   Bg4   Nd7
       1.   Nf3 – e5 +

The knight forks all three Black pieces, gaining the bishop next move. Black's knight can't defend because it's pinned.

246 W: Kg1   Bh4   Pf4   Pg4   TRAPPING
       B: Kh7   Bg6   Pf7
       1.   f4 – f5

The pawn attacks the bishop, which is trapped and lost.

247 W: Kf3 Rf7 Bb4   SKEWER
B: Ke8 Nb8 Bb3
1. Rf7 – f8 +
Supported by the bishop, the rook skewers king and knight.
The knight is lost.

248 W: Ka2 Qd2 Pa3 Pd3   FORK
B: Kd8 Ra8 Rh1
1. Qd2 – g2
The queen forks the rooks. Neither can move to defend the
other. White wins a rook.

249 W: Ke1 Qg1   PIN
B: Ke8 Ne5
1. Qg1 – e3
The queen pins knight to king. The knight is lost.

250 W: Kg1 Qd4 Rd1   PIN
B: Kd8 Bb6 Nd7
1. Qd4 × b6 +
The queen takes the bishop. The knight can't take back
because it's pinned.

TEST **26**

(Answers 251–260)

Black to move

251 W: Kh2 Qc2   DISCOVERY
B: Kc8 Rg3 Bc7
1. ...   Rg3 – c3 +
The rook attacks the queen, discovering check from the
bishop. The queen is lost.

252 W: Ke2 Bg2 Ne4   PIN
B: Kd7 Qe6 Pf7
1. ...   f7 – f5
The pawn piles on the pinned knight, which is helpless to
defend itself. White loses material.

253 W: Kg2 Bg5 Nb5   SKEWER
   B: Kg8 Ra8 Pg7
1.   Ra8 – a5
The rook skewers knight and bishop, winning one of them.

254 W: Kf7 Qh3 Bg7   DISCOVERY
   B: Kc6 Qc8 Nd7
1.   . . .   Nd7 – e5 +
The knight checks, unveiling an attack on the queen. White
wins the knight, but Black gains the queen.

255 W: Ka1 Bb1 Na2   MATE
   B: Kd5 Bc1 Nd1
1.   . . .   Bc1 – b2 + +
The bishop sneaks in and mates.

256 W: Ke3 Pe7   FORK
   B: Ke1 Ra5
1.   . . .   Ra5 – e5 +
The rook forks king and pawn, winning the pawn next move.

257 W: Kb3 Nf3 Pe3 Pc3   FORK
   B: Kb7 Qg7
1.   . . .   Qg7 – f7 +
The queen forks king and knight, garnering the knight.

258 W: Kf3 Rh3 Pa6   PROMOTION
   B: Ka8 Pg2 Pc6 Pa7
1.   . . .   g2 – g1(N) +
Black promotes to a knight, trades knight for rook, and soon
gets a new queen. If Black first promotes to a queen (without
check), White's rook checks and then mates.

259 W: Ka1 Qe5 Bh2   X-RAY
   B: Kh8 Qg7 Ba7
1.   . . .   Ba7 – d4 +
The bishop forks king and queen, with x-ray support.
White's queen is lost.

260   W: Kd1   Rb1   Bf1   MATE
          B: Kd5   Re2   Nd3   Pe3
          1.   ...   Re2 – d2 + +
The rook mates, supported by the pawn. The knight guards two potential escape squares along the edge.

TEST **27**

(Answers 261–270)

Black to move

261   W: Kf1   Qg1   Re1   MATE
          B: Kf3   Nb1
          1.   ...   Nb1 – d2 + +
The knight mates, with the aid of Black's king, the gatekeeper.

262   W: Ka2   Qg2   DISCOVERY
          B: Ke6   Qg8   Bg6
          1.   ...   Bg6 – b1 +
The bishop checks, uncovering an attack on White's queen, which can't be salvaged.

263   W: Ke4   Bf1   Pf4   FORK
          B: Kh4   Rg4   Pg5
          1.   ...   Rg4 × f4 +
The rook takes the pawn with check, forking king and bishop. The bishop is lost.

264   W: Ke1   Rh5   Be3   DISCOVERY
          B: Ke8   Rb5   Bc5
          1.   ...   Bc5 – b4 +
Black's bishop checks, uncovering a winning attack on White's rook.

265   W: Kb2   Rg7   Bg6   PIN
          B: Kg2   Qh1
          1.   ...   Qh1 – h8
The queen pins rook to king. The rook is lost.

266 W: Kg1 Qb1 Nb2 MATE
B: Kb3 Qh3 Bb8
1. ... Bb8 − a7 + +
The bishop mates from a distance. Black's queen shuts the gate.

267 W: Ka4 Qa3 Ba5 MATE
B: Kc4 Pb7
1. ... b7 − b5 + +
The pawn mates, under the king's guidance.

268 W: Kf2 Bb2 Pd2 FORK
B: Kd1 Rd3
1. ... Rd3 × d2 +
The rook clips the pawn with check, giving a winning fork.

269 W: Kh1 Nd2 Ne2 Ph6 SKEWER
B: Kh8 Rf6 Ph7
1. ... Rf6 − f2
The rook skewers the knights, winning one of them. This is better than taking the pawn with check.

270 W: Kg6 Rc2 FORK
B: Kc6 Bg2 Pc5
1. ... Bg2 − e4 +
The bishop forks king and rook, winning the rook. Black will soon make a new queen.

TEST **28**

(Answers 271–280)

Black to move

271 W: Kh1 Qh2 Pf2 Pg2 MATE
B: Kf1 Ng4
1. ... Ng4 × f2 + +
Knight takes pawn mate.

272 W: Ka1 Rc2   *EN PRISE*
         B: Kd1 Qd3
         1.   ...   Kd1 × c2
         Take with the queen and it's stalemate: a draw instead of a
         win.

273 W: Kc1 Bc5 Pb6   PIN
         B: Kg8 Qg2
         1.   ...   Qg2 – c6
         The queen pins the bishop to the king. The bishop is lost.

274 W: Ke2 Ra6 Pc4   FORK
         B: Kc8 Be6 Nf1
         1.   ...   Be6 × c4 +
         The bishop takes the pawn, forking king and rook, defending
         the knight, winning the rook.

275 W: Kh4 Rh3 Bg4 Ph5   MATE
         B: Ka4 Bb4 Ne4
         1.   ...   Bb4 – e7 + +
         The bishop mates. The other check doesn't do it.

276 W: Kh2 Qa8 Bb7   DISCOVERY
         B: Kh7 Rb2 Bg2
         1.   ...   Bg2 × b7 +
         The bishop takes the bishop, attacking and winning the
         queen. It can do this because of the rook's discovered check.

277 W: Kc5 Bd3 Pd4   DISCOVERY
         B: Kd7 Rf5 Pe5
         1.   ...   e5 – e4 +
         The pawn advances, attacking the bishop and uncovering a
         check from the rook. The pawn takes the bishop next move.

278 W: Ke1 Nh5 Pg4   TRAPPING
         B: Kb5 Be2 Be5
         1.   ...   Be2 × g4
         The light-square bishop takes the pawn, winning the knight
         because it's trapped.

279 W: Kd7   Nh3   Pd4   FORK
        B: Kf7   Bb3   Pf4
        1.   ...   Bb3 – e6 +
The bishop forks king and knight, winning the knight. Black
soon makes a new queen.

280 W: Ke8   Re7   Bd7   MATE
        B: Ke1   Rf7   Ne6
        1.   ...   Rf7 – f8 + +
Protected by the knight, the rook mates.

TEST **29**

(Answers 281–290)

Black to move

281 W: Kb1   Rc1   Rf8   MATE
        B: Kb3   Bf6   Nf3
        1.   ...   Nf3 – d2 + +
The knight moves in and mates. Black's king and bishop
take care of loopholes.

282 W: Kg1   Rg4   Ra1   DISCOVERY
        B: Kf6   Qh8   Pf4   Pf7
        1.   ...   Kf6 – f5
The king attacks one rook while discovering a queen attack
on the other. White must lose a rook.

283 W: Ka1   Bh6   Nb6   DISCOVERY
        B: Kd4   Rd8   Bf6
        1.   ...   Kd4 – c5 +
The king attacks the knight and the bishop discovers check.
The knight is lost.

284 W: Kh1   Bh7   Ng1   PIN
        B: Ka8   Qa1
        1.   ...   Qa1 – h8
The queen pins the bishop to the king and wins it next
move.

285 W: Kg5 Ra5 Ba2 Bd2 Pg2 FORK
B: Kd1 Qd7
1. ... Qd7 × d2 +
The queen takes the bishop with check, forking king and rook, and winning the rook.

286 W: Kh1 Bh2 MATE
B: Kh8 Bh7 Nh3
1. ... Bh7 − e4 + +
The knight traps, the bishop mates.

287 W: Kh1 Rf1 Bd1 Pg2 MATE
B: Kd5 Rh5 Nh2
1. ... Nh2 − f3 + +
The knight moves, blocking the bishop, while uncovering a mating rook check.

288 W: Kc3 Qg7 Pe5 FORK
B: Ke4 Bc7 Pg5
1. ... Bc7 × e5 +
The bishop takes the pawn, forking king and queen. The queen is lost. Black wins the endgame.

289 W: Kh3 Re6 Nd1 Pd7 PIN
B: Ka7 Qa4
1. ... Qa4 × d7
The queen takes the pawn, pinning the rook and winning it next move. This is better than taking the knight.

290 W: Kh1 Rd2 Rc1 Pc2 SKEWER
B: Kc6 Qh8 Bh5
1. ... Qh8 − h6
The queen skewers both rooks. White has no defense. Black wins at least a rook.

TEST 30

(Answers 291–300)

Black to move

291 W: Kb4   Bf4   Pd6   PIN
       B: Kd7   Qd8
       1.   ...   Qd8 – h4
The queen pins the bishop to the king. It's a dead issue.

292 W: Ka5   Qd1   DISCOVERY
       B: Ka8   Rh5   Bf5
       1.   ...   Bf5 – g4 +
The bishop attacks the queen and shields the discovering
rook. Black gets the queen.

293 W: Kf6   Qf7   DISCOVERY
       B: Kd8   Rd6   Ne6   Ph6
       1.   ...   Ne6 – g5 +
The knight, protected by the pawn, attacks the queen while
unveiling the rook's discovered check. The queen goes.

294 W: Ka1   Rf5   Bb5   Nb1   Pa2   MATE
       B: Ke5   Rf1   Bf6
       1.   ...   Ke5 × f5 + +
The king takes the rook, unmasking mate.

295 W: Kf5   Rd5   Ne4   Pe6   FORK
       B: Kc8   Rc6   Pb7   Pd7
       1.   ...   d7 × e6 +
The pawn takes the pawn, giving a forking check. White
loses a rook.

296 W: Kf8   Na6   Nc8   Pb7   FORK
       B: Kh8   Rh6   Bc6   Pg7
       1.   ...   Bc6 × b7
The bishop takes the pawn, forking the knights. One will
cease to exist.

297 W: Kd3 Bg6   SKEWER
B: Kd5 Bd1 Na3
1.   ...   Bd1 – c2 +
The bishop checks. The king must move. White's bishop is seized.

298 W: Kd1 Qe2 Pd2   PIN
B: Kg1 Rg4 Bh5 Ph4
1.   ...   Rg4 – g5
The rook unveils the bishop's pin, while protecting the bishop. The queen is lost.

299 W: Kh1 Rf1 Bb5   MATE
B: Kh4 Rh5 Ne2
1.   ...   Kh4 – g3 + +
The king moves up and out of the way so the rook can mate.

300 W: Kf6 Pe6 Pg6   MATE
B: Ke8 Rh8 Nc6 Ph6
1.   ...   0 – 0 + +
A good life. Castle and mate.

TEST TABLE

Under SCORE indicate the number of correct answers achieved in that particular test. Keep a running total under CUMULATIVE SCORE. Check level achieved in the Test Results appendix.

TEST	SCORE	CUMULATIVE SCORE
1		
2		
3		
4		
5		
6		
7		
8		
9		
10		
11		
12		
13		
14		
15		
16		
17		
18		
19		
20		

TEST	SCORE	CUMULATIVE SCORE
21		
22		
23		
24		
25		
26		
27		
28		
29		
30		

TEST RESULTS

CUMULATIVE SCORE	LEVEL OF ACHIEVEMENT
Under 50	**Rank Beginner** You have either just learned or just forgotten how to play.
51–100	**Novice** You've been playing for a while, but haven't had instruction.
101–150	**Intermediate** You play regularly. You win some, you lose some.
151–200	**Advanced** You're a frequent player. You've read at least one chess book.
201–250	**Tournament Player** You could be a contender.
251–275	**Graduate Student** You could show, place, and even win.
Above 275	**Master Class Level I** You've been taking private lessons.
Above 275 (At no more than 10 seconds per problem)	**Master Class Level II** You've been giving private lessons.

ABOUT THE AUTHOR

BRUCE PANDOLFINI is the author of fourteen instructional chess books, including *Pandolfini's Chess Complete; Chessercizes; More Chessercizes; Checkmate; Bobby Fischer's Outrageous Chess Moves; Principles of the New Chess; Pandolfini's Endgame Course; Russian Chess; The ABC's of Chess; Let's Play Chess; Kasparov's Winning Chess Tactics; One-Move Chess by the Champions; Chess Openings; Traps and Zaps; Square One;* and *Weapons of Chess.* He is also the editor of the distinguished anthologies *The Best of Chess Life & Review,* Volumes I and II and has produced, with David MacEnulty, two instructional videotapes *Understanding Chess* and *Opening Principles.*

Bruce was the chief commentator at the New York half of the 1990 Kasparov-Karpov World Chess Championship and in 1990 was head coach of the United States Team in the World Youth Chess Championships in Wisconsin. Perhaps the most experienced chess teacher in North America, he is co-founder, with Faneuil Adams, of the Manhattan Chess Club School and is the director of the New York City Schools Program. Bruce's most famous student, six-time National Scholastic Champion Joshua Waitzkin, is the subject of Fred Waitzkin's acclaimed book *Searching for Bobby Fischer.* Bruce Pandolflini lives in Manhattan.

TACTICAL TIPS

1. **Know the Board:** Learn the name and color of every square. Try to visualize the beginning and end of each rank, file, and diagonal. Mark where they converge. Look for connection points. As you walk with friends, discuss squares and lines.

2. **Study Related Opening Tactics:** Familiarize yourself with typical shots. Fix in your mind key avenues of attack. Trace how the pieces get there. Make a mental list of standard pitfalls in your chosen openings. Practice exploiting them. Play systems with similar attacks so that all experience is relevant.

3. **Think in Patterns:** Study thematically. Note winning forces, their arrangements and interactions. Be sensitive to similar designs in your own games. Close your eyes. Feel vectors and force fields, harmony and peace.

4. **Classify and Save:** If you see a usable tactic, make it yours. Delineate it. Compare it to others you've seen. Try to think of analogous positions from your own play. Diagram it or photocopy it. Put it in a notebook or on index cards. Organize by theme. Be creative. The more personal, the easier to remember. Read tactical books that group by concept. Note unforgettable names. Make them up.

5. **Solve Problems:** Do tactical puzzles incessantly. Read through books with composed or real game situations, arranged thematically or randomly. Both is best.

Work from diagrams. No need to set up positions on actual chessboards. Use time limits. If you exceed them, you lose. Lose daily.

6. **Do It In Your Head:** Always analyze without moving the pieces. Pretend it's a real game. Worthwhile exercise: Study a book diagram for ten seconds, close the book, and try to set up the position on a real board. Do this often and you'll see deeper and quicker. When analyzing, use algebraic notation in your internal monologue. If you become confused, start the analysis over, no matter how many times it happens. Never give up on a problem. Take hours. Take it with you. You're worth it.

7. **Play Sharp Openings:** Risk losing. You'll learn more. Play gambits and opening sacrifices. This will force you to be resourceful. Acclimate to tactical terrain and other harsh realities.

8. **Play Speed Chess:** This helps you concentrate on threats and attacks, honing tactical skills. Get a partner. Play dozens of speed games from favorite openings or problem positions. Then check analysis. You'll learn faster. But don't do blitz before tournament games. You'll lose faster.

9. **Study Games of Attacking Players:** Kasparov, Tal, Alekhine, Marshall, Keres, Spassky: Their games are rife with brilliant tactics and combinations. Emulate the best. Be like them.

10. **Analyze Complicated Positions:** The more complex the better. Assign an analytic hour. Do it in your head, time yourself, and write it in a notebook before checking. Repeat. Now and then, look back and smile.

TACTICS GLOSSARY

Attraction   The forcing of a defending unit to an exploitable square.

Back-Rank Mate   A mate given by a queen or rook along the first or eighth rank. Also called a *corridor mate* or a *back-row mate*.

Battery   Two pieces of the same color attacking along the same line supportively.

Check   A direct attack on the king.

Checkmate   The situation of having no legal move when the king is in check. The end of the game.

Combination   A forced series of moves, usually involving sacrifice and often blending several tactical themes, which leads to a definite improvement in position.

Decoy   A stratagem that lures an enemy unit to an area or a particular square.

Deflection   The forcing of a defending unit from its post.

Discovery   An attack by a stationary piece unveiled when a friendly unit moves out of its way. Also called *discovered attack*.

Double Attack   Any attack against two separate targets simultaneously.

Double Check A discovery in which both the moving and stationary units give check.

En Prise Referring to a unit that is attacked and undefended.

Fork A simultaneous attack by one unit against two enemy units.

Gambit A voluntary sacrifice, usually of a pawn.

King Hunt A series of moves that chase the enemy king around the board until it is mated.

Mate Short for *checkmate*.

Mating Attack A general assault against the king, leading to mate or significant material gain.

Overload A situation in which a unit cannot fulfill all its defensive commitments simultaneously.

Piling on Exploiting a pinned unit by attacking it with additional force.

Pin An attack on an enemy unit that shields a more valuable unit.

Pin Overload Exploiting an overloaded unit by pinning it.

Promotion Advancing a pawn to the last rank and converting it into a queen, rook, bishop, or knight.

Sacrifice Generally, the offer of material for some other kind of advantage, such as initiative.

Shut Off   A line block that prevents an enemy unit from controlling or using a rank, file, or diagonal.

Skewer   The opposite of a pin. A line attack on a valuable unit that by moving off the line exposes another unit in capture.

Stalemate   A drawn game. The situation of having no move but not being in check.

Strategy   A general plan.

Support Mate   A mate given by a unit that is protected by another.

Tactics   Immediate attacks and threats.

Technique   Getting the most out of a position by precise maneuvering, with attention to nuances and subtle moves.

Trapped Piece   A piece with no escape that can be attacked and captured, usually with advantage.

Trapping   Leaving a piece with no safe moves, so that if attacked the piece would be lost.

Undermining   Destroying a unit's protection by capturing or driving away. If it's done by capture, it's also known as *removing the guard* or *removing the defender*.

Underpromotion   Promoting a pawn to a rook, bishop, or knight, but not to a queen.

Unpin   A counterattack that breaks a pin, gains time to break a pin, or ends it by eliminating or diverting a pinning unit.

X-ray   Two friendly pieces supporting each other for defense or attack along the same line, separated from each other by an enemy piece of the same power.

TACTICS INDEX

(NUMBERS REFER TO PROBLEMS)

If you'd like to work on specific kinds of tactics, for learning or review, this index will enable you to find them by group.

DISCOVERY

EN PRISE

FORK

MATE

7	10	11	16	22	29	34	35
46	49	50	51	55	62	70	72
78	82	89	93	99	102	109	119
120	122	129	138	140	147	148	155
160	164	166	174	178	183	189	191
196	200	205	206	214	220	224	225
231	236	239	241	242	255	260	261
266	267	271	275	280	281	286	287
294	299	300					

OVERLOAD

3	36	38	69	86	108	121	132
145	162	208					

PIN

2	8	14	20	21	37	43	44
53	64	76	79	84	90	96	105
112	125	130	134	142	156	161	168
175	180	184	188	202	212	217	226
249	250	252	265	273	284	289	291
298							

PROMOTION

27	73	128	151	207	258

SKEWER

5	17	28	33	45	52	59	61
71	83	92	94	106	110	113	114
126	135	143	150	153	176	186	190
195	199	203	213	218	227	228	238
247	253	269	290	297			

INDEX